Manipulation and Dark Psychology

How to Learn the Techniques to Influence People with Persuasion, Mind Control, NLP. Why it is Necessary to Know How to Use Manipulation for Empathic Relationships

By

Paul Jones

Table of Contents

Introduction

This is not just a book - it is an arsenal book. It describes quite serious and powerful techniques that can change both your life and the lives of those with whom fate brings you. Among other things, I wrote it with a shock of my own sincerity, describing the mechanisms of influence as they are. Uncensored. So - without fuses.

So I recommend to remember: these are not toys. You can really get from people what you could not before. You can really influence them even at the level of their well-being. You will understand how easy it is to make a trance and how easy it is to instill the ideas and motivations you need. Therefore, it is better even for gaming or training purposes to give only those suggestions that you yourself would not refuse.

I made a decision to write openly consciously. The fact is that all of us, one way or another, constantly influence both ourselves and others. And with words, and gestures, and facial expressions, and intonations ... So the question is not whether to influence or not to influence. The question is, do you know what influence your words and actions have. And do you want to change something in them when you know their true meaning? Ethics is not a refusal to manipulate, but a conscious choice of ethical goals for manipulative skills.

Dark psychology is a promising area of modern practical psychology that is actively used in NLP technologies. It is based on simple and easy-to-learn verbal techniques that allow you to influence your interlocutor and achieve success in any areas of activity: negotiations, sales, advertising, marketing, personnel management, personal relationships.

This is not just a book - it is a trainer book. She does not just inform - she teaches. I tried to make you get the most out of it. Even with inattentive reading. Reading it, you will at times immerse yourself in a trance, where you will receive and learn all the necessary teaching suggestions. The book will provoke you to emotions, to a dispute with me or with the authors I cite. Everything is good. So, it is conceived.

Individual sentences may go beyond the grammar of the basic English language, yet, everything is correct. The laws of neuro-linguistic programming, dark psychology and manipulation dictate their own ways of dealing with words. And it is quite possible that all these nuances will be noticed only by the editor, but not by you.

Some topics and thoughts will be repeated more than once. Sometimes in the same words. At the first reading, I recommend just to believe: it is necessary. The second reading will give you several times more information: you will already understand what and why I am doing in this book. A third reading will show that the bottom here is not double, but triple.

And at some point, you will find that you too can. And perhaps you will be surprised that you once thought that it was difficult. Yes, yes, everything is that simple. And I'm not a magician, but just as human as you are.

I illustrated some thoughts with jokes. I would like to hope that thanks to the examples suggested here, you can learn all about manipulation and dark psychology much faster. A wealth of knowledge around! You just need to know where to look. In fact, I am going to teach you all of these in this book.

Paul

Chapter 1:
What Is Dark Psychology?

Any person who has ever fed a baby from a spoon has induced an easy trance on them. First, you take a spoon and stir the porridge. Then, you pick up porridge in a spoon and meet your eyes with a child. Your breathing is even fine. What do you do next? You need to put the porridge in the baby's mouth. You open your mouth, and the child does the same—and you hold out the spoon.

Dark psychology is an applied area of Ericksonian hypnosis. Is it all clear? Not for everyone. Therefore, we will deal with each spoken word.

Dark psychology is the technology of introducing a person into a state in which he cannot or does not want to resist our influences. Let's say he likes us so much that he is ready to listen to any nonsense, or he is so disoriented that he does not follow the nuances, or he sees in us the only way to his salvation—whatever it may be. There are many options. Dark psychology techniques are a way to provide us with such joy.

The Erickson hypnosis is a direction developed by students of the greatest hypnotherapist of the XX century—Milton Erickson. He managed to refute the myth widespread in those days that there are people who are immune to hypnotic effects—say, who has cool willpower that cannot be hypnotized. Erickson charmed everyone.

The essence of his method was that Milton Erickson used not one specific method of hypnosis but a whole palette of tools. Therefore, if one of them did not work as it should, the doctor moved on to the next faster than others could notice his mistake. Someone compared the work of the master with the work of an "intelligent cracker."

Fortunately for us, this turned out to be not a property of a genius but a technology independent of the master, which anyone can learn. True, identifying the nuances of this technology required quite the painstaking work of Erickson himself and his students. The greatest merit in this matter belongs to Ernst Rossi and the founders of neuro-linguistic programming (NLP): John Grinder and Richard Bandler.

Thus, dark psychology techniques can be considered not only the direction of Erickson hypnosis but also one of the NLP models—Milton Erickson's model of hypnotic work—or, as they say in NLP, the Milton model.

The fact is that although Milton Erickson himself used his hypnotic abilities mainly for psychotherapy and training, the communication model separated from the source showed its highest efficiency in completely different areas. The Milton model works in public speaking, in sales, in negotiations, in collaboration with superiors, or in the management of subordinates—in a word, wherever we need to get something from other people.

What you plan to master is not a panacea for all ills. This is just a tool—with its capabilities and limitations. A highly qualified specialist will achieve excellent results with its help. The successes of beginners are obviously more modest.

And one of the secrets of mastery is to know in advance. It can be formulated as: "A nail fitted in furniture with a screwdriver holds worse than a screw hammered in with a hammer," or "Do not stick square sticks in round holes." In other words, manipulation and dark psychology techniques should be used where it is most effective, and it should not be used where it does not work.

Actually, this book is devoted to the description of these subtleties and nuances.

Chapter 2:
Dark Psychology Traits —
Presuppositions of Manipulation Tactics

Presuppositions are basic assumptions—prerequisites. They are in NLP. And by the way, the basic presuppositions of NLP also work in dark psychology. However, there are several prerequisites that are important precisely in speech exposure. I propose to talk about them now. Fortunately, no one has done this before us. I hope that being aware of the basic presuppositions of dark psychology, you better understand the techniques of speech exposure and NLP themselves.

Here is a list of presuppositions of dark psychology and manipulation:

- Behavior is determined by the subjective reality.

- Trance is a natural and habitual state.

- Most of the behavior is unconscious.

- Incomprehensible attracts attention.

- Incomplete action seeks completion.

- The unconscious understands only the language of images.

Behavior Is Determined by Subjective Reality

- Do I really have the ability to do magic?

"Do you know what magic is?"

- The art of changing the world with words.

"Right. And why can words change the world?"

- I do not know. This is a secret, probably? Needing special words?

"Special—" the fact is, my boy, that the world is just an idea of people about it.

Each of us lives in two realities: objective and subjective. The objective is the reality of physical objects. It is measurable, continuous (without holes), and each of its objects has a past and a future (nothing appears from nowhere; nothing disappears anywhere). According to objective reality, it is convenient to coordinate behavior, as for two different people, it is one.

With subjective reality, it is more fun. Everyone has their own— although, of course, there are intersections. In subjective reality, there is that which is not in objective because it is created by words. Harry Potter, corporate culture, respect, karma, sin, goal-setting, neuro-linguistic programming—all this is not in objective reality. However, they feel quite comfortable in the subjective, despite their apparent non-physicality.

Moreover, the very concepts of objective and subjective realities are by no means objective—they exist only in my (well, yours now) subjective reality. However, objectively, there is no subjective reality. On the other hand, there are obviously objective external differences between the Chinese, Koreans, Vietnamese, and Japanese—but I wouldn't try to determine so on the spot. Subjectively for me, there is no external difference between them—not an obvious one, at least. It is similar, however, that it is not obvious to them that my face is very Icelandic and not American or Canadian—yes, and for you, most likely.

Now, let's proceed with the most important thing. What reality depends on what a person will do? It seems paradoxical, but human behavior is determined not by objective but by subjective reality—and objective only in that part in which it intersects with the subjective.

If you do not notice the cold, you will not be wrapped up. If you are not aware of the financial crisis, you will not panic and will not withdraw your money from the account. If you do not agree to take colored papers as money, you will not do anything for them.

On the other hand, if you believe that you will be paid for the scrap metal by weight of gold, you will run around and collect pieces of iron throughout the city—even if it turns out to be a joke. If you think that indoor plants harmonize the flow of vital energy, you will look after them, and the energy will be harmonized—whatever it means.

If you see only two alternatives, you choose only between them. Obey or quit, for example. If you see the third, you will choose between the three. Objectively, in the next room, there may be a bomb that will explode in 30 seconds—but if you did not believe me, you continue to sit here and read these lines. Objectively, a glass of water in the morning may prolong life for 35 years—but those who do not believe in this do not check.

Behavior is determined by the subjective reality. If you understand brands and models of cars, you see that cars are different—if not, the same. Subjective reality is drawn in words. Actually, that's why dark psychology is generally possible. You can talk to a person so that he is himself! Voluntarily, we will do what we need. Marrying, obeying, working for free, fidelity to store, help, buy, give discounts, recommend us to friends—all this (and everything else) is determined by subjective reality, which we can influence with the help of words—if we do it skillfully.

Trance Is a Natural and Habitual State

There is nothing unusual in a trance. Trance is a state when a person thinks one thing and does another—distracted, just put. The opposite state of trance is awareness when conscious attention is focused on actual actions and events. On the other hand, fixing attention on a specific object, we unwittingly get distracted from everything else. Therefore, trance is also a state where our attention is focused on one thing.

As you can see, most states fit the definition of trance. Every time we focus not on the actual task but on our thoughts, we are in it. Whether in memories, in fantasies, in reasoning, or in experiences, we are in a trance. Every time we focus only on an urgent task, we are also in it: when we watch TV, read, eat, or work.

They say that in trance states, the brain works differently. Some areas are activated, while others are muffled. The illogical right hemisphere comes to the fore—logic falls asleep. They say that in these minutes, the doors to the unconscious open, and the possibility of change appears.

How do you determine that you are in a trance? In order to do this, focus on the internal signs of trance:

- Narrowing of the focus of attention

- Missing part of external information (fragmented perception)

- Change in perceived body temperature

- Relaxation

- Inability to control their own actions

- Unwillingness to move

- Distortion of perception of time

- A stopped look

- Loss of focus

- Rich internal images

In a word, this is everything that we often call the word "thoughtful" (and also "lost his head," which is even more interesting for our purposes). It is useful to track these symptoms in your own home to use the magical power of self-hypnosis—or to return to awareness. It is useful for the interlocutor to inspire them so that the trance deepens.

From the point of view of manipulation, trance is very convenient in terms of impact. If a person is immersed in emotions, he has no time to test our logic. Thinking of something of his own, he lets holes in the argument. Re-experiencing the events of the past, he may not hear some of our suggestions. Consciously, the unconscious will still hear and will accept for execution.

It is clear that trance is one of the natural states of man—and some even claim that trance is necessary for survival. In particular, it is short-term trances that allow us to restructure our internal experience in order to adapt to an ever-changing reality. That is why when people are faced with troubles or surprises, they are temporarily immersed in a trance. Thanks to trance, we find comfort—and each return from a trance is a meeting with a more pleasant state than before—unless, of course, the opposite was suggested.

Surely you noticed behind yourself that every one and a half to two hours, for some time, it becomes more difficult for you to focus on work, and there is a desire to plunge into yourself. This is a natural trance. If you do not resist this urge, after ten to twenty minutes, your batteries will recharge, and your working capacity will be restored. New ideas will come, inspiration will appear, and a "second wind" will open—you have rested.

A person is very often in a trance. Every time the "outside" is too boring, he plunges into his thoughts—and *this* is a trance. Every time "outside" becomes scary and / or uncomfortable, many of us "hide" in a trance just like ostriches. Every flash of emotion is a trance—a condition in which practically nothing depends on consciousness—it is in touch. Dreams, reading, TV, computer, a long trip, and routine activities are everyday sources of natural trance states.

Every day, trance interlocutors need to be noticed and used, as it is precisely at these moments that they are open to your suggestions. How do you notice this? A trance has characteristic external signs, and if you are careful enough, you will notice that people in a calm trance experience the following:

- Vision is defocused

- Eyes are stopped

- Pupils are dilated

- Muscles are motionless

- Breathing is changed

- Blinking is slowed down

- Jaw droops

- Body is relaxed

In a word, they look like falling asleep. However, the exact opposite of these external signs is also suitable for us. It is characteristic of vivid emotions, and it is difficult not to notice them. It is also important to understand that not all people show all the signs of trance at once. Therefore, it is more important to see the desired trend in order to strengthen it using appropriate techniques.

What then? The simplest thing we can do, having noticed that the interlocutor has plunged into himself for a while, is to forward a suggestion—that he could "reject" or dispute if he would follow our words more closely. We take the conversation to more solid ground, and as soon as the interlocutor was distracted—the next "forwarding."

Forwarding can be a command for the future, the necessary interpretation of the fact, not very well-founded judgment, the desired information—and all this, with the same intonation, with the same facial expression, under the motto, "Nothing happens." We do not need the interlocutor to pay attention to our forwarding. On the contrary, we want him never to remember that he heard from us like that—and the more we forward in the right direction, the better the final effect.

Most Behavior Is Unconscious

It is easy to make sure that any action that we do is quite elegant and is controlled not by consciousness but by the unconscious. In order to do this, just come to any sports section and try a new movement. Reception, dance step, acrobatic element—out of inexperience, you will do it consciously, which means that it's rather clumsy.

Awareness of habitual movements is a fairly serious meditative practice. To breathe consciously, to consciously walk, to consciously raise one's hand, to speak consciously—all this is a big job. And of course, we do not tear like this in our daily lives. Here's another!

Moreover, we push off on the autopilot and more or less regularly recurring sequences of actions. Traveling from home to work and back is unconscious. The absorption of food is often unconscious. Cleaning the bed is automatic. Essentially, these are routine work operations.

A platoon of marines came to the cinema to watch a Hollywood action movie.

At the climax, the heroine kills her lover with a pistol and asks in a tragic voice:

"Well, what am I to do now?!"

Commander's voice from the audience:

- Inspect the weapons and move beyond the firing line!

This is very convenient because by pushing a large part of the usual routine onto the autopilot, we release consciousness for more important (from his point of view) tasks. Hence, while arms and legs control the machine, eyes control the surrounding area, and ears listen to the radio—an experienced driver can additionally think about plans for the day and maintain a conversation with passengers. It seems like conscious action, although the selection of words, intonations, and facial expressions still have to give up to the autopilot.

We program our unconscious, and it already carries out the tasks assigned to it, thus controlling our body, emotions, and thoughts. This, however, is a rather optimistic statement because firstly, not everyone knows how to program their autopilot efficiently, and secondly, it is not just us who sets the programs— even so: basically *not* us.

Whoever wanted something that was well-advertised by television or friends? And whoever discovered that he could not cope with an unconscious impulse to do what the consciousness would not want to do—or, on the contrary, not be able to force yourself to do something? The unconscious rules.

Why is this useful in dark psychology? Even if a person is consciously against it, it is enough for you to agree with his unconscious, and the thing will be done at that moment when consciousness is distracted—and, by the way, a person may not even notice or remember that he fulfilled your suggestion. Well, nice! The main thing for us is to get the result.

Incomprehensible Attracts Attention

The unknown is painful for people. Frankly, it scares them! And everything that scares automatically attracts attention. An unfamiliar word—*what is it?* Unusual action—*why is it?* Strange behavior—*why is this?* Violation of the familiar sequence—*why would it?* We need to deal with all this and find an explanation for everything. While there is no explanation, a person is dominated by a state of discomfort—of uncertainty. Everything is clear—*a relief*—and you can live on.

You could not use this property of the human psyche, as fixing attention is a trance, and distracting attention from your suggestions is also good. Therefore, if you manage to confront a person with the unknown (to confuse him), a trance is guaranteed. All this can be done in a very ordinary conversation! It would be a desire.

The classic method of creating confusion is breaking expectations. The fact is that people's behavior is saturated with rituals, patterns, and stereotypes. Everything is subject to public and unwritten rules, and people implicitly expect others to fulfill them: rules of etiquette, traffic laws, subordination, corporate culture.

We do certain actions and expect to receive the given reactions in response. Holding out his hand, we are waiting for a handshake. Asking a question, we expect to get an answer. Giving a gift, we look forward to gratitude. We expect all interlocutors to be related to the topic under discussion. We expect that before the conversation, there will be a greeting, and after, a farewell—*expectations, expectations, expectations.*

Violation of any of the stereotypes causes confusion. And if at the same time, the intruder behaves as if everything is in order (i.e., he can neither be accused of insanity nor be suspected of joking), the confusion intensifies. Attention is reliably fixed on the search for an explanation of what is happening—and if at this time, the suggestion is forwarded, it passes conscious control unnoticed. The man will not even remember this—especially if then you still give an explanation that will suit him, and his inner watchman will calm down.

For example, husband and wife are sitting in the evening, watching a horror movie. Suddenly, a monster appears on the screen.

Wife: "Oh, mommy!"

Husband: "Yes, it seems."

Man seeks to understand. Therefore, he will look for a match for your words in his experience and beliefs, remember what you refer to, fit in your head all your complex sentences with numerous conjunctions and inserts, and clarify terms and concepts unfamiliar to him—provided, of course, that in principle, he is interested in delving into your words. However, having gained the desired clarity, a person calms down and stops thinking.

Therefore, if we, on the contrary, do not want to draw too much attention to our words, we try to make our speech as predictable as possible. Intonation transitions are smooth—no jumps in volume and speed! The general intonation pattern of speech is calm—all is well, and nothing is happening. Some monotony, in combination with the wave-like voice, lulls very well.

Something similar can be said about content. If you do not want to attract too much attention, speak just and clearly—like with a child. It is believed that the unconscious intellect is at the level of a 5- to 7-year-old child. Hence, say it clear—no complicated words, no complicated designs—everything is simple, all clear, in pictures, in metaphors, in the images, in black and white, with no mid-tones, literally. When you talk to people like that, they calm down.

Once again. Incomprehensible attracts attention. If you want to attract and hold attention, speak/do what raises questions. Do you want a person to be distracted? Perform just the opposite, and let your behavior be as predictable as possible. If you want to be given the opportunity to talk for a long time, use unfamiliar words—and in response to a request to clarify, do explain. While you explain, all the trump cards in your hands—because you are talking, and he is listening.

Incomplete Action Seeks Completion

If a person started something, he definitely wants it.

Unfinished business causes a feeling.

Partly, it's because the brain remembers every unfinished.

Have you felt it?

Here is another example. What do you think is shown in this image:

It's a triangle and a circle, isn't it? That's not true. This is a broken line and an arc. Take a closer look: they are incomplete. However, the brain wants to complete them. One would like to say: *an incomplete triangle, an incomplete circle— almost a triangle, almost a circle. I want completeness!*

This is a fundamental property of the human psyche—and with your permission, I will complete the proposals that have been started. If a person started something, he definitely wants to complete it, as unfinished business causes a feeling of discomfort—the brain constantly draws on the ending, tells what just needs to be done. This is partly due to the fact that the brain remembers every unfinished business, which means it spends part of the actual attention on it.

In particular, psychologists found out that the conditions of the begun but unsolved problems are remembered by students for a long time. Similarly, the waiter remembers the orders on those tables where they have not yet paid. Everyone who went to the store for shopping, keeping in mind that he needed to buy, remembers that having paid, he easily forgot his list.

How is it used in manipulation and dark psychology? It's very simple. If you started to tell a story but did not finish, it now takes a part of your conscious attention. When you finish it, the part of the conversation that has wedged between the beginning and the end of the story will be forgotten. For fidelity, however, you can invest up to a dozen stories in one another. Many techniques for structuring amnesia are built on this.

If you raised a topic but did not discuss it fully, a person will think about it himself when you are not around. If you prompted a person to start doing something but did not let him finish, he will continue as soon as possible. The funny thing is that oftentimes, a simple story about action is enough for a person to want to do it himself later. However, it is better if it is not completed in the story—or it will end not as the listener would like. Promises without fulfillment also motivate: first to promise, and then postpone for various good reasons—and desire is growing! Incomplete action seeks completion!

On the other hand, it is important to make sure that a person does not begin to resist you—because if he started, he would want to continue. It's better to lose quickly: "No, no, no. I'll do it myself—or I'll offer others." However, these are already extreme measures. It is better not to give cause for resistance at all, acting gently and imperceptibly, in the spirit of subtle manipulation.

The Unconscious Understands Only the Language of Images

- Just remember, no stupid newfangled meters and centimeters—no numbers! Can you visually imagine eight and a half centimeters?

- No.

- That's all. Speak figuratively, and do not use numbers. You are not giving the blacksmith a task. You do magic! And magic—it is built from pure beauty, from the magical harmony of words!

If a picture, sound, sensation, smell, or taste is behind your words, the unconscious will understand you. No. Unconscious thinking is often associated with the work of the right hemisphere of the brain. These are images, emotions, associations, premonitions, and specifics of experiences—and they are not at all logic, numbers, sequences, and abstractions, as in the left.

Therefore, we communicate with the unconscious just. As with a child, I remind you: "an apple," "tasty," "eat" — this is understandable and unconscious. *"I believe it will be useful for you to eat this fruit; it contains vitamin C."* This is for consciousness. Moreover, if you say something like, "You are probably well aware of the fact that you have some obligations to your family, so it would be right if you helped us somehow—for example, by giving money," the unconscious will understand the main thing: "Give us (the family) money." The rest for him is noise.

To be honest, that's how we understand words—translating them into images. Even if these are abstract mathematical formulas, they become vivid and understandable only if a suitable picture is behind them—and if there is no picture, the word is incomprehensible.

A classic example here is the perception of unconscious words with negatives. Behind the word "loser," there is usually a picture—however, for the phrase "not red," there's none. Therefore, if in the first case, the unconscious understands that it is a loser, in the second, it will remember the red color.

Remember, if you need to negotiate with the horse and not with the rider, you need to stock up on the carrot that the horse loves and not poke it with the money that the rider loves. The unconscious loves pictures—draw with words. In the end, we are required from a person, not something abstract, but rather concrete behavior. Go where we need to. Sign the paper. Give us a nod in the right place. Make a smile at our appearance. The specific behavior expressed in the pictures—here, we draw them!

Suggestions are modes of action—unfinished, in the future, and then when necessary. A suggestion is what is understood by the unconscious—what a person is able to perceive in a trance when his right hemisphere of the brain is activated, and the left is slightly euthanized. A suggestion is a direct appeal to an unconscious person—that is, to the one on whom it really depends, the person will do what we need, or will not.

In the same way, with auto-suggestion, communication is with one's unconscious. Only here it is even simpler. You can do without the mediation of words—just imagine what you want or the desired action—incomplete, in the future, and forget it. Then, the unconscious will do what you need—because he will understand, and thereby, it is programmed.

And so that everything worked for sure, it's useful to know that the more often the desired picture flickers before your eyes, the stronger your inner desire to do what is visible on it. Therefore, to instill the desired behavior, a key image is often selected, and it is called repeatedly. Do you have to wash the dishes? Easy! *"I washed the dishes today. Thank you, by the way, that you often help me and wash the dishes! You know, I'm so pleased when you decide to wash the dishes. When I see how you wash it, I feel that you care about me. Your hands washing the dishes are so strong and gentle! When I wash the dishes, I often remember with tenderness your hands."*

And that's it! Now, we change the subject so that the action remains incomplete.

Chapter 3:
Psychological Manipulation Techniques

All effective actions have the same structure—a sequence of stages—the absence of any of which dramatically (sometimes to zero) reduces the likelihood of success. The impact, built clearly on this structure, is triggered with the greatest possible probability—true, not one hundred percent. The impact, I repeat, refers to any and in any field—in politics, in business, in personal relationships, in sports, in war, in religion. If the effect worked, you are very likely to find a familiar structure in it.

This miracle is called a single impact structure. A single impact structure can be described in two languages, each of which is useful:

- Background lines

- Stages of exposure

Background Lines

So, whatever our goals, if we want to influence another person (or group of people) successfully, we must build three lines of communication:

- Contact line

- Line of distraction

- Line of exposure

Contact Line

Contact is an opportunity for mutual exchange of information. Contact is a desire to perceive each other. Contact is the assumption that communication is more beneficial than ignoring. If there's no contact, nothing—therefore, the mainline is the line of contact. It begins earlier than all; it ends later than all.

Since it is precisely we who are interested in establishing contact, we are doing everything to make it appear and be present throughout the communication. We find time for a meeting, we call up, we try to be noticed, and we dress and talk so that we are agreed to be distinguished from the general background—and even when a person "escapes" from communication, he thinks, "Is it not that I run too fast?"

Any advertisement should contain "contact information," the one on which the proposed product or service can be found—at least, with the help of a search engine.

If the advertisement is new-fangled and contact information has not yet been offered, it means that the seller prefers to keep in touch with you through his advertising media. A telephone and address will be offered later. This also corresponds to the structure.

Conversely, when a person is afraid that the impact of the other side will be more effective than his, he can just break the contact—so debtors avoid meeting with creditors, so passers-by try to get around street vendors and gypsies, so many business people refuse to watch TV, so children run away from home to not be invited to dinner, so weak fighters try to escape from the enemy, running around the edge of the tatami.

However, contact is not only important for this. Through the contact line, we receive information about the interlocutor's reaction to our influences: feedback. And based on this information, we correct our behavior. Actually, this is one of the main differences between a literate communicator and an ordinary communicator—a literate one notices when he is mistaken and quickly fixes what needs to be fixed.

What the interlocutor likes, what he agrees with, what worries him, what he hides—he will tell us everything—not a word, so a body. Generally speaking, our line of contact pertains to the line of influence of the interlocutor on us. It depends on him what we will do next. The words of the interlocutor give us the key to how to communicate with him—appearance, emotional reactions, the appearance or disappearance of signs of trance, changes in his posture and breathing—*open only your eyes and ears!*

Distraction Line

A man is designed so that his first involuntary reaction to a direct offer or request is a refusal—anyway, any new information. Outwardly, he may not give a look, but he is internally tense. (Track, by the way, your reaction to these allegations. Did you agree at once?) Then, after thinking and weighing the pros and cons, he can make a positive decision—but inexperienced communicators by this time may already leave upset.

We all unconsciously strive for the same thing—to maintain the status quo, so that nothing changes, to make everything familiar, and so that there were guarantees that tomorrow would be like yesterday—because we are already used to what we have. Let us live in a swamp, but it is ours and is familiar to the last bump. Here, we can easily get rid of any enemy—but we won't fight back, so we'll hide in a pre-prepared assortment. Therefore, the reaction to change is appropriate—*wary*.

And all this goes by the mind—involuntarily—that is, quite reasonable, logical, profitable ideas and suggestions pass by. In the sense of being eliminated, it is rejected at distant approaches. And few are able, having thought it all over again, to return to what he himself had sifted out. Therefore, even when we offer a person a truly valuable transaction, point of view, or information, we have to introduce a line of distraction.

In other words, in order to act effectively, it is necessary to distract the "internal controller" of the interlocutor. Well, about the same as if you wanted to get into a guarded building—you first have to deal with his guard. Say the password, show the pass, arrange for him a "call from above," sell to pity, bribe him, shy away with a baton, or blow up an explosion packet at a neighboring entrance, finally. In a word, it is reliable to neutralize until we finish all the machinations we need.

How do you distract the "controller"? For example, the interlocutor's consciousness goes on a mental journey through the past or future, which we will arrange for him. Do you remember the charm of the words, "Do you remember," and the stories of, "Beautiful far away?" Likewise, let the "controller" get carried away with the struggle with the flow of information, fall into an emotional whirlwind, live in a fabulous reality, and listen to our explanations. (All this and much more are ways of inducing a conversational trance.) Let him be distracted. Because while he is watching, we cannot do anything worthwhile. In the meantime, the "controller" is resting—we will work—and keep in touch with this!

Line of Exposure

When there is contact or when the interlocutor's consciousness is reliably distracted, a line of influence may appear—fragmentarily, imperceptibly, and always ready to hide even more reliably. On this line, we inspire—throw ideas, form the necessary attitude, suggest suitable interpretations, motivate, awaken desires—*the main work is ongoing.*

It is clear that the vast majority of suggestions are indirect. Yes, we are not impudent. We act just where we are not resisted. We do not suggest, "Give us all the money." We explain, "It's not just a cactus but a big-money cactus," and therefore, this cactus costs "only five thousand American dollars." We are not saying that the person needs to obey everything; we only make it clear that in the prevailing—*terrible!*

And I remind you: the line of action is fragmented. Most of our words are either reliable or unverifiable in the current conditions. However, our suggestions are forwarded: there is a not quite logical combination, and there is not a completely substantiated statement. Here, we say "possible," and after a couple of sentences, "only possible." Here, the word in one sense; there, in another. Likewise, for example, you can create a mood with one story, and then transfer it (there are special methods) to another—and all this briefly, forwarding, no pauses, continuing to speak, without stopping the speech flow, taking away attention away from "slippery places."

The second feature—all forwarding work for the same purpose, inspire the same thoughts—let the wording be different, but their essence is one. Thus, an outwardly ordinary conversation with all the usual paraphernalia turns out to be filled with a dense stream of suggestions that work for a given purpose.

At this moment, all three lines are simultaneously involved: impact, distraction, and contact—but *that* is the essence of a single impact structure.

Stages of Exposure

If you need to know about the three lines of communication necessary for success in order to understand the essence of a single impact structure, for practical use, it is useful to consider it as a sequence of stages, each of which is necessary and sufficient in its place.

How to move from lines to stages? It's very simple. If you project the background lines on top of each other, it turns out that there are five key segments in a single impact structure:

- Fixation of attention

- Depotentialization of control

- Intervention

- Latent period

- Synchronization

The presence of each of them is mandatory. The absence of any of them can ruin the effect on the root—and it is clear that, without finishing the previous one, it is impossible to move on to the next. However, now, the difficult task of holding two or three background lines at the same time turns into a clear step-by-step scheme, from which it is clear what to do and why.

Fixation of Attention

Attraction and retention of attention—without it, no impact on a person is possible. For if you did not attract his attention, you, for him, are not—and nothing can affect. Therefore, the first active step in any manipulation algorithm is to fix attention.

Hence, the goal of the stage is to attract and capture the attention of a potential interlocutor so that it turns from potential into reality. To begin with, you provide yourself with the opportunity to be seen and heard. In order to do this, you can:

- Be in plain sight;

- Appear in a personal area (approximately 1.5 meters from the body);

- Say hello;

- Contact by name;

- Offer to talk;

- Offer to look at what you show;

- Ask for a moment of attention;

- Sometimes, touch;

- And so on.

However, it is not enough to attract attention—it is also necessary to *keep it*.

The attraction of attention is similar to wrestling capture—after it, reception is possible—and experienced fighters, by the way, are fighting precisely for the seizure, as the rest is a matter of technology. Then, you can make a trance, "powder your brain," and offer the interpretations we need. There is attention; they listen to you.

Attention must be attracted—and attracted attention must be retained (and in case of distraction, returned). In other words, to be effective, you must be able to attract attention constantly, over a given period of time, and then let go, and become invisible—you need to be able to do this, too.

What attracts attention?

- And the first thing that comes to mind here is *values*. Recognition, wealth, power, freedom—the list of values is extensive and unique for everyone. However, if the conversation offends your values, this is an important conversation—and your attention will remain on him.

- Farther. What else is important? Right! *Needs*. If you are hungry, you involuntarily catch any information about food. Even the names of the dishes attract attention—and if the nose catches a smell, obviously, the attention will go there. Sexual need—if you are not just after long stormy sex, the appearance of a sexually attractive object will interest you. And so on: there are many needs.

- The following are *emotions*. Joy, fear, enthusiasm, anger, tenderness—I don't know why, but what is said emotionally attract an order of magnitude more attention than what is said dryly. Exceptions can be made only when usually emotional speech suddenly becomes dry and flat—but this is to the next method.

- *Change.* Any changes in the world around us are an occasion to test them for possible danger. It is in instincts. Therefore, a change in the rhythm of speech or gestures; a change in volume, speed, or pitch of a voice; transplantation and movement; a change in the topic of conversation—all these attract attention—for a while. And then, you need to change this something again.

- And the last thing that comes to mind is *consistency*. All the same, instinct encourages people to look around for support—those they can trust, those that look like us— therefore, a person sitting in a similar pose, breathing in the same rhythm, speaking with consonant intonations, attracts attention—and, of course, unconsciously.

In general, the attention of an untrained person completely follows these decoys involuntarily. And therefore, it is far from always consciously—just because most people are not accustomed to controlling their attention.

We will talk more about attention in more detail, but now, remember any clip, any advertisement, or any TV show. How often does the picture change there? Ten or more times per minute? Now, guess why? Right! It is to fix your attention while they inspire you with everything!

Depotentialization of Control

I used to talk about this stage as a distraction of consciousness. The practice has shown that this is not entirely true. The fact is that if you work honestly (i.e., you suggest that for which a person will then be grateful to you), it will not be conscious resistance that will hinder you at all but the dullness of his unconscious.

Prejudice, beliefs, inertia of thinking, instinctive resistance to the new, stereotypes learned decades ago, and banal laziness—all this forms a fairly rigid network of control that does not allow almost anything to human consciousness.

So a direct appeal to a reasonable and conscious part of the interlocutor is often our goal. Further, the man himself will "understand his happiness." Well, if for some reason you want to create something that is more advantageous to you than him, then you will have to depotentialize (lower the resistance potential) not only unconscious resistance but also the possibilities of his consciousness.

Hence, the goal of this stage is to enter into trust and cause a trance state of the interlocutor. That is the very state in which he cannot or does not want to resist our influences. How to do this is further written. Here are techniques for tuning, and techniques for causing confusion, and conversational trance, and the use of decor. In a word, humanity has developed a huge potential for depotentialization. Potentially, you can use it.

Intervention

The purpose of the stage is to quietly forward the necessary suggestions, weaving them into the context of communication. At the same time, I remind you, while maintaining the capture of attention and depotentialization of control! A particular art here is the selection of goals for suggestions.

As you already know, we often inspire a completely different topic than talking. This is additional insurance against the interlocutor's resistance, and has the assurance that they will not be able to "catch us by the hand": we were talking on a different topic!

A competent manipulator does not try to inspire direct actions like, "Surrender to me this night," but the prerequisites for them are, "Take everything from life," "What romantic music," "You can trust me," etc. There is even a separate type of indirect suggestions built solely on hints, the conclusions of which are made by the manipulated person—the right conclusions.

There's one more point related to interventions that we have not mentioned yet. There must be many suggestions—up to several dozens in one meeting. Do we care about increasing the likelihood of the desired outcome for us? Hence, we act like missiles with multiple warheads: can one intercept and shoot down one missile, and when it is divided into a dozen? More difficult, and accordingly, it is easier for us.

Latent Period

The latent (hidden) period is processes that are invisible to us within the interlocutor. He recalls something, compares, imagines some pictures, somehow convinces himself—he embeds our suggestions in his system of choice and decision-making. During this time, our suggestions become his own views—opinions, preferences, beliefs, etc. However, these internal processes are also most often hidden from the interlocutor himself—and we contribute to the best of our ability.

An agricultural conference is taking place.

The Frenchman gets up:

- We sow potatoes on May 15, and we harvest on September 16.

The Englishman gets up:

- We sow potatoes on April 15, and we harvest on August 16.

The Chukchi rises:

- We sow potatoes on June 15, and we harvest on June 16.

They ask him:

- In one day? Why so early?

- I really want to eat!!!

This stage of a single impact structure is the quintessence of a hypnotic approach. We sow and water, but we never pull the stems in the hope that the seedlings will sprout faster! We want a person to do what is required of him, himself. Voluntarily. It is desirable, with enthusiasm. And in order for this desire to mature in him, it takes time. Therefore, conversational hypnosis is always a job for the future.

In this place, I want to distract myself from saying that the master of conversational hypnosis is befitting three virtues: modesty, politeness, and patience.

- Modesty is the habit of working "out of the shadows," influencing indirectly, without sticking out your contribution to the heads of others. Modesty prolongs life. And it allows you to not really answer for anything.

- Politeness is the ability to ask for just what a person can give painlessly. Plus, polite language, of course. This is the essence of all indirect suggestions. Politeness also prolongs life. More precisely, it does not give a reason to shorten it.

- Patience is the ability to wait. Ability to think in advance. The ability to not rush anywhere. Exactly because, by the way, everything was thought out in advance. Patience helps to be humble and polite.

Therefore, after we have completed the intervention phase, we need some more time to "confuse the tracks."

The purpose of this stage is to divert the interlocutor's attention as far as possible from the fact of the impact, so that the interlocutor, with all the desire, could not remember what was suggested to him. We continue the conversation without much change in intonation or posture. We do not allow ourselves to breathe a sigh of relief or to cast a victorious glance at our interlocutor. Our motto is, "There was nothing!" We are just continuing.

As a bonus, at this stage, it is useful to instill amnesia, i.e., make the listener forget most of the conversation. I mean, I only remembered the most general and safest things for us. This, for example, is facilitated by a sharp change in the topic of conversation closer to the end of the latent period. In addition, the techniques of shaking, confusion, overload, boredom, and other types of trance are at our service. You will read more about them.

Synchronization

Psychologists figuratively distinguish three stages of change: defrosting, modeling, freezing. Potters have a similar story: clay softening, molding, firing. And specialists in systemic NLP identify the same stages in changing systems and organizations: destabilization, change, stabilization in a new center of equilibrium. So we are doing the same: we removed control, put in a new picture of the world, and in the end we return control.

What for? Everything is simple and clear: we want the changes we have introduced to be preserved. Do you remember the conservative forces within each person? At first, they interfere with us, so we try to weaken them, but when we have done everything, we want the same forces to help us, sacredly guarding the results of our work!

Chapter 4:
Blinding Persuasion Technology with Neuro-Linguistic Programming (NLP)

The Trust

Trust is a willingness to accept a person's words on faith—that is, without prior verification. Trust is irrational by definition because it is a rejection of rationality. It is based either on a person's perception of "their own" or "reliable" or on the expectation that since he has not failed several times, he will not fail now—which, of course, is not necessary at all.

One of my acquaintances told me something that happened at his workplace (a research institute). An unfamiliar guy comes up: he asks for an eraser, takes it, and leaves. After 5 minutes, he returns with thanks. After a while, he asks for a fountain pen— and also returns. Then, he asks for a tester (an electrical appliance quite expensive at that time), receives, and leaves— this time, for good.

Of course, trusting, we substitute. No one can truly guarantee that this particular "very decent" man will not turn out to be a scam, and this "seventh generation intellectual" will not stick a knife in our backs. In the same way, it is impossible to guarantee that the "decorous" lady does not have such a hobby as participation in group orgies.

But without trust in our life is no way. Firstly, it's because a person with an adequate (!) level of paranoia is guaranteed a place in the ward for the mentally ill. Secondly, it's because suspicion requires an increase in decision-making time, and modern life is accelerating more and more, and people who can solve quickly are in demand—and risky, of course. Thirdly, the amount of resources is limited, and if you have invested most of them in your security, there will be few resources left to move towards other important goals for you.

In a word, you have to trust. But in order not to be mistaken very often, people use the criteria by which they determine whether this particular stranger can be trusted. There are three of them:

- Image and role - How does a person dress, move, and speak? What are his accessories and visible attributes? How do other people feel about him? What is known about him from available sources of information? In a word, from what circle is he.

- Similarity - How does this person look like me? Do I understand his words? Does he share my point of view? Am I comfortable with him? Do I keep up with him, and does he slow down? Does he understand my feelings and emotions? In a word, as far as I can predict his actions.

- Communication experience - Did he fail me before? Did you keep the promises? Did you say the right thing? Did we have serious contradictions? Did you give any explanatory advice? In a word, did he deserve my trust?

Knowing these mechanics, we can maximize our chances for people to start trusting us at least so that our verbal (speech) suggestions work out to strengthen this trust. And, of course, the tools offered further are the beginning of non-verbal (non-speech) suggestions. So far, focused on one narrow, but extremely important topic—trust.

Image and Role

Fortunately, or vice versa, people are not able to interact directly with your soul or thoughts. Therefore, they have to rely on your facade, that is, on what you voluntarily or involuntarily flaunt. This is convenient for us in that we can (again, more or less) manage all this and use it for our own purposes.

Role Expectations

Any wizard who has mastered the difficult science of teleportation knows: it's not enough just to move from one city to another, in the blink of an eye to be on top of a mountain or on the seashore. It is also important to ensure that all witnesses to the movement are fully aware—how difficult this process was and how strong the wizard who created this.

One young magician, for example, moved in parts. At first, the feet appeared on the ground, then the knee, hips, stomach, chest, and neck—only at the last second did the head appear from the void. Another wizard, older and more impressive, appeared all at once, but at first, he was transparent, colorless, then became black and white, then slowly acquired color.

A famous sorceress, who visited the co-duchy a couple of times in her wanderings, came out of the silver mirror that appeared in the air, which was supported by tiny colorful birds. At the same time, fragrant lilies of the valley streamed from the sorceress's hair, and luminous pollen flew from her hands.

Another illustrious sorcerer, an old and stern man, came out of the air surrounded by flames, his clothes were often torn, his magic wand glowed with a crimson light, and in his other hand the sorcerer clutched a bloodied dagger—it appeared that the sorcerer's path was only in sight quick and simple, but in fact he walked in secret hellish paths, fighting along the way with countless monsters.

What someone asked a question about teleportation, he received an honest answer—all these beautiful things have no meaning and are an illusion designed to delight and intimidate the witnesses of witchcraft.

Dark psychology and manipulation. This is a skill. And its application needs context. Where do you plan to apply your skills? In the management of subordinates? In negotiations with potential business partners? In sales? In communication with persons (and bodies) of the opposite sex? For public speaking and presentations?

Strangers interact at the role level. Each person can play many roles, but only in some, he will be convincing enough to inspire confidence in himself. The flimsy bespectacled man is hardly suitable for the role of a dominant male. A girl in a vanishingly short mini is not suitable for the role of an experienced psychologist, no matter how wise she is. As well as a gray-haired power aged man will be inadequate as a foreman at a construction site.

It depends on whether your image is suitable for the role you have declared, and whether you will be trusted in this role. This is especially important when a person already has role expectations in relation to you. If I am a business coach, I must look and behave accordingly—in a suit, smart, clear, brisk. If I am an ideal subordinate, my behavior should also change—attentive eyes, tenacious memory (or notebook), specific remarks.

A brightly played role—this is a suggestion—an incentive to take a complementary role.

A crow is sitting on a tree. A rabbit is jumping by. He saw a crow, stopped, and asked: "What are you doing?" She: "Yes, what I want—so I'm not doing anything." Rabbit: "Can I do this?" Crow: "Why not?" The rabbit sat under a tree, sitting, doing nothing. A fox ran past, looking: a rabbit was sitting. Then, she ate it.

Moral: "To sit and do nothing, you need to be able to sit very high."

What should you do to be perceived in such a way that it does not stop you from getting what you want from people? Among the roles that you want to play (giving the desired effects), you must choose those that you—really—play easier.

How to bring yourself in line with the selected role? Find samples and copy. Literally—you are looking for the best in your chosen role and studying everything that is available: how it moves, how it speaks, how it dresses, how it makes decisions, what it prefers, etc. Discard excess then.

Personal Myth

A personal myth is what people think and tell about you. A piece of alien subjective reality. The myth is because it has too little to do with reality, even if you set out to tell the truth about yourself, and only the truth, and even wrote an autobiographical book, true. People will come up with it anyway.

Your myth goes ahead of you, forming people's expectations at your expense. It can clear the way for you. It can create many obstacles in your way. It may be easy for you to match it, or it may be that you will constantly disappoint people in their expectations. In any case, people have (at least some) myths about you in their heads, and it would be nice for them to manage consciously. This is especially true for those who communicate with new people a lot.

There are four sources of your myth:

- What are you telling? These are your stories about yourself, i.e., stories about what happened to you. It is possible and fictional, but believable, i.e., fit into your role. If they are cool or interesting, they will be remembered and retold. Just remember that stories must be such as to create the right myth about you—the one that is convenient and necessary for you. And suggestion patterns will be your feasible help in this.

- What others are saying about you - People who have a lot of money and/or friends may not tell stories about themselves - others will do it for them. But suggesting what you can tell about and what you should be silent about is useful—even with the help of non-verbal suggestions. Of course, if there is a sea of grateful people around you, they themselves will tell you everything about you. But this element is sometimes useful to manage.

- How you look - It would be funny if it were not for everyday reality for many. "Throw dust in the eyes." Most often, they do this when they are going to seduce another client or a carcass of the opposite sex—a car bought on credit, watches that are borrowed from a wealthy relative, "mother's lipstick, older sister's boots," an office with an hourly rental. Plus, you can wash, shave, scent, or hold your back up. The hope, as usual, is that people tend to generalize a single experience. Well, or you can gradually get all this for yourself in constant use. Or reconcile with the level of claims to which you really correspond now.

- How do you do? The solid component of your myth, reputation, is formed from your actions. And here I have only one recommendation: keep your promises. Otherwise, from time to time it is necessary to abruptly "change the habitat," escaping from one's own shadow. But when you gain a reputation as a reliable person, you can allow yourself to look as you like, not to control the myth, in a word, to be yourself.

A man in the bazaar sells parrots—one on his head and one on each shoulder.

Customer:

"How much is this bird (pointing to the one sitting on his left shoulder)?"

- 3000 euros.

"Why so expensive?"

- In addition to being an English speaker, he also knows higher mathematics and chemistry.

"How much is this (pointing to the right)?"

- 5,000 euros.

"Very expensive!"

- What do you want? In addition to higher mathematics and chemistry, he is fluent in English, French, and German!

"And this one, then (pointing to the one that sits on his head)?"

- 10,000 euros!

"What does he know?"

- I don't know what he knows, but the other two call him the boss.

And the last thing that is currently useful to note when speaking about personal myths. Myth is an inertial thing. Therefore, if you are going to form it consciously, be prepared that it will be difficult to stop the overclocked composition. Letters still come to me with questions about personal relationships, although I myself have not been interested in this topic for several years. Choose a myth that will not be a burden to you in many years.

Recall, by the way, the favorite of millions of Arnold Schwarzenegger, from whom, even at the age of sixty, they expect him to portray a dashing fighter against terrorists in films. Or look at the sad action movie about boxer Rocky Balboa, who, even being old and sick, was still forced to expose his head to the blows of another young rival.

The wife enlightens her husband:

- According to the rules, makeup should be done this way: first, you need to wash your face with foam or use a scrub, then wipe your face with tonic, bring a moisturizer, foundation, foundation, well, and spray the powder.

- Why all this?

- To get a natural complexion.

Congruence

Congruence is a good combination. When different aspects of your facade say the same thing, each with their own means. Accordingly, incongruence is a combination of unsuccessful, contradictory. A smile with drooping shoulders, sneakers with a business suit, a furious cry: "Stop yelling!" Any incongruence is a sign of falsehood and an occasion to trust in a less frequent manner—and we want to trust us more.

What should correspond to what?

- Verbal and non-verbal signals - Simply put, what you say and what you demonstrate with your body. Say, when you say that you are glad to a person, and the jaws and fists are clenched at the very same place, you are not trusted very much. And do not trust accordingly. "Vigorous - we must speak more vigorously, cheerful - more fun. Non-verbal suggestions should strengthen verbal!

- Sense and logic - Here, we must try so that you do not contradict yourself, the observed facts and logic very clearly. People forgive each other for minor flaws, but if you lie - we will call a spade a spade - brazenly, they will not trust you. Do you need this? It is necessary to speak in such a way as to catch you on the contradictions was difficult. We will learn this soon.

- Various nonverbal channels - This is when the arms move at a different pace than the whole body, or when the right-hand gestures noticeably more than the left, or when the voice is loud, and the gestures are mean, or the voice is high and slow at the same time, or when unloaded muscles are tense. All this suggests that a person still does not believe in himself—and how can we believe this?

- Clothes and accessories - Single style, color matching, close-price category—you must admit that a tracksuit with patent-leather shoes looks rather strange, with an expensive phone with a worn, dirty jacket, and a chic belt with a home dressing gown. Here, the examples are extreme, but also smaller discrepancies make you think.

- Myth, image, and role - This is written above. Here, I only emphasize that all aspects should support and strengthen each other. Well, you yourself understand that.

A lady comes to dry cleaning:

- You know, for many years I couldn't meet a man. I probably don't attract anyone with my gray dress. Repaint it, please, in red color.

The lady gives the dress to the receiver and leaves. An hour later, a joyful woman runs in:

- In red—do not! Repaint in white!

An hour later, she enters, sobbing:

- Repaint in black.

The receiver mutters to himself under her breath:

- That's what can happen in two hours if you go outside without a dress.

Congruence comes naturally enough when your life is orderly. In other words, when all aspects of your life support and reinforce each other, the same thing is projected outward. This is most reliably done by working on our internal conflicts and problems, and NLP provides a fairly rich toolbox for this purpose.

Fine-Tuning

Adjustment is a demonstration to a stranger that you are "of the same blood" with him. You are just like him. Trust here arises from the illusion of your predictability. Say, if I understand him, if he looks like me, then I know how he will behave in certain circumstances.

A policeman stops a car with a blonde behind the wheel:

"Your rights, please."

- What?

"Rights, please."

- And what are rights?

"This is such a thing with your photo."

- Ahhh! - The lady delves into her purse, takes out a mirror. - You are welcome.

A policeman looking in the mirror:

"Well, why didn't you immediately say that you are a policewoman?!"

On the other hand, this is a way to make it more convenient for a person to communicate with you, so he had to think less—that he had to strain less. Accordingly, he becomes more relaxed, more open, and less attentive and thoughtful—that is, he is one step away from the desired trance.

In short, fine-tuning is a wonderful tool for a manipulator. Another thing is that when adjusting, it is important to remember that role relationships are still primary. It is not necessary for a man to dress in a dress in order to adjust to the desired woman. It is not necessary for the doctor to groan in suffering, mirroring the patient. It is not worth the sports coach to copy the motor habits of a beginner. Trim should not interfere with the role!

Body Tuning

The easiest mirroring option. What I observe, I repeat. This is how it works in life. Look at any pair of people who relate to each other, and you will be surprised how much they are alike! Their movements are coordinated, their voices are coordinated, and their views are coordinated. And the style of clothing is usually agreed upon.

And vice versa—if people conflict or argue over issues of principle, coherence disappears somewhere. And it already looks like a cacophony of an orchestra without a conductor—with deaf musicians.

And in fact, the task of bodily mirroring is not even to cause involuntary, unconscious trust, as is often taught in NLP courses, but to not "squander" the excess. That is, the minimum task is to at least not push the person away with your non-verbal. And for complete trust, we will enhance the effect by other means.

The four most important points in body tuning:

- Adjustment of the pace of movements and actions

- Tuning according to the pattern of muscle tension

- Breath adjustment

- Fine-tuning according to voice characteristics

Pace

The pace is the speed of a person's life—speed of movement, frequency of change of action, speed of decision-making, the length of sentences in speech, the brightness of emotions, the dynamics of the development of relations, the presence or absence of preludes in conversations, or the number of events per unit time.

The life of a city dweller is faster and richer than the life of a villager. Capital residents are faster than provincials. And the speech, of course, is not about who runs fast, but about who thinks faster and more efficiently—because life is like that.

Accordingly, the first rule of any coordinated activity is that the pace must be agreed upon. Agree, it is inconvenient to carry the piano when one loader goes faster than another. And it's inconvenient to talk along the way when the interlocutors go at different speeds. And any technological chain will break if people have a different pace of work.

So it is necessary to issue information at such a speed with which a person manages to assimilate it or at least write it down. And ask questions at a pace so that you have time to answer. And it is desirable to move so that you have time. This is later—after you have gained confidence and begin to use psychological overload techniques, you will deliberately speak and act faster. But at first, it's good that a person at least decides to have business with you.

But what if the person you are talking to is faster than you? Here is only one piece of advice: learn to think and act in advance as quickly as possible. Expand your comfortable speed range, in other words. By the way, those who think in pictures quickly think. So learn.

Pose

A person's pose is, in many ways, are an expression of his emotional state. It is determined by the pattern of muscle tension. Agree: a person who is completely relaxed and a person who is very tense feel, to put it mildly, in different ways.

Accordingly, if you manage to copy the interlocutor's pose, you enter approximately the same state that he is in. They pulled their heads into their shoulders, hunched over, put their hands together, sat down uncomfortably—one condition. They raised their heads, breathed deeply, relaxed their hands, sat down more conveniently—another.

It is important to remember: in principle, it is not the external resemblance, but what muscles are tensed now. It is difficult to sit on a stool in the same position in which it is easy to be in a chair. It's difficult to portray a seated person. But to tighten up the same muscle groups is quite possible—and get a similar internal state, which is required.

Because at that moment, you begin to understand the person—and he feels it and is imbued with sympathy and trust—so it works. I do not know why; it just does.

At the same time, when you have achieved a similar state, you cannot get carried away with further imitation. That is, you can hold a position that is convenient for you, taking care only that the identity of experiences is maintained. And which leg is thrown over which leg, you scratch behind the ear or straighten the hair—this is your business.

Breath

Breathing is another key to a person's internal state—subtler and more powerful. Here, you will already need a fair amount of observation to notice the interlocutor's breath.

The simplest thing you can do with information about the interlocutor's breathing is to breathe in the same way as he does. In the same rhythm, with the same depth, in the same way. And you will get a similar internal state.

True, on one condition: you must be physiologically similar. For example, it's natural for children to breathe much faster than adults, so the normal rhythm of a child's breathing will probably seem to be quickened for an adult. And the yoga's normal breathing rate may well euthanize an untrained person.

Therefore, it is better to adapt to the breath of a person who is very different from you, not directly, but crossly. Well, for example, shaking his foot in the same rhythm. Or nodding your head slightly at each exhale. Or something like that. The point here, however, is no longer in similarity, but in the ability to control the state of the interlocutor. But more on that later.

Confidence, by the way, can also be strengthened in this way.

Voice

In our culture, people pay little attention to how their voice sounds, so it gives an untrained person "giblets." The interlocutor can arbitrarily portray confidence with correctly set gestures, posture, and gaze, but if he has a choked or monotonous (or even trembling) voice, it is clear to us: the person is worried.

Any bodily characteristic has feedback with the body. Simply put, we can influence our internal state by changing its external manifestations. Not ultimatum, but noticeable enough. It is this effect that is used in tuning the body and breathing. We will use it with voice tuning.

The voice has many characteristics, and each of them can be used to enhance the confidence of the interlocutor.

- Speech speed - Everything that we talked about when discussing the pace of a person is true here. Speaks quickly - thinks quickly; thinking slowly - slowly speaking. If you want a person to keep up with you, speak at the same speed as him. Hear someone speaking quickly, be sure: he will expect the same from you.

- The volume of the voice - With all other things being equal, the volume sets the distance in communication— both literal (the farther the person is, the louder it is necessary to speak so that he hears), and metaphorical (the quieter the voice, the more confidential the communication). In this sense, it can be useful, starting with the volume suggested by the interlocutor, gradually lowering it, starting to speak quieter, more confidentially.

- Intonation - The tone and pattern of the voice is a fairly substantial part of the image of a person. It is one thing if he speaks in a muffled and monotonous manner—quite another if his voice plays with all the colors of the rainbow, shimmering and transforming every second. The tweak here is a demonstration of the proximity of roles and statuses. What is important, it is extremely rarely recognized, but quite effective.

It is clear that listening to the voice of the interlocutor, and even more so, managing your own will for some time, be unusual and uncomfortable. But the more valuable the prize: you can adjust so that no one will notice it. And this is especially true in our time when NLP techniques are known to many.

Verbal Adjustment

No matter how important the non-verbal adjustment is, one cannot deny the fact that the correct selection of words also affects the effectiveness of communication. At least in terms of understanding. An extreme example is a conversation with a foreigner: you can match both in style, in the internal state, and in voice nuances—while you use obscure words, it's difficult to count on understanding.

Similarly, it is difficult for children to understand adults. Adults - teenagers. Ordinary people - scientists. Entrepreneurs - experts. Why? The language is different. And without understanding, there is no trust. And in general, there is nothing, to be honest. However, in order for a person to do what is required of him, it will be enough for us to create the illusion of understanding. How this is done, now let's figure it out.

Hungry wolves met one hare in the forest and were about to eat it, but the hare tells them:

"Wait a minute, you won't get enough of me, but I can lead you to a flock of sheep."

The wolves decided not to eat the hare and went after him. They go, and hunger torments more and more, they ask:

- How long do we go?

The hare answers them:

"Here, right behind the mountain in front of us."

They began to climb the mountain—the wolves could not cope with hunger, attacked the hare, and ate. They didn't get too full, hunger torments, but there is no more temptation before their eyes. They climbed the mountain and saw a flock of sheep.

"We had a hearty lunch," and then one of them said:

- Somehow, it turned out badly with a hare.

Other:

- Yeah, come on, are we going to bury the remains?

They returned, buried the hare, put a stone on the grave and thought: What to write? "To a friend hare" - it won't go; they won't understand why his friends ate him.

"Enemy of the Hare" - also will not go; what kind of enemy is he when he brought them to the herd of sheep?

They thought and wrote: "To our consultant and partner - a hare."

Keywords

If you carefully listen not to what a person is saying, but to how he does it, you can easily find the obvious thing: people tend to highlight those words that seem to them to be key. The very ones in which the very essence of the utterance is laid.

For example:

- *It would be great if you HELPED me.*

- *It would be very healthy if you could help me.*

- *It would be great if YOU helped me.*

Agree, quite different meanings are obtained! In the first case, help is more important to a person, in the second—the fact of help itself, in the third—the response of you specifically. And you need to respond differently to these three different requests. If in the first case, you can invite someone who will help instead of you, then in the latter the main thing is to come in person.

How to use the knowledge of the interlocutor's keywords? Very simple: your answer should contain these words. Then, the person will be sure that you are listening to him. And you see. If he says that "Mom brought Pies yesterday," you answer about pies. If he unknowingly identifies the word "mother" in the same phrase, then the answer is about the mother. And what about "yesterday"? The answer is obvious, isn't it?

By the way, relatively recently, I suggested that the participants in my training do the opposite. That is, to communicate, as it turns out, but with one small change: in their answers, there should have been a systematic absence of the keywords of the interlocutors. Synonyms—it is possible. The words themselves are not. The result exceeded even my expectations: the people almost quarreled!

Perceptual Predicates

One of the rather important characteristics of the interlocutor is which system of perception - vision, hearing or sensations - he currently prefers. This is expressed both on a non-verbal level (in the choice of clothes, in the pace of life, in the pose in gestures, etc.), and in what words a person expresses his thoughts.

It's one thing when he says something like "Your arguments resonated in my soul; it's nice to hear ideas that are consonant with mine." It's completely different when he presents his position in the spirit of "It was easy for me to find a solid foundation under your position." I hope you clearly saw in these phrases those shades that I wanted to show you. In the first sentence, there were words indicating the auditory system of perception. Meanwhile, the second was composed of kinesthetic (sensory) words. It is obvious that there are also visual words.

Examples:

- Visual: clear, picture, perspective, see, bright, violet, lens flare, spot, prominent

- Auditory: tone, quiet, fret, loud, voice, speak, consonance, ring, echo, creak

- Kinesthetic: warm, soft, deliver, recoil, wedge, tension, iron, warm

Accordingly, it will be easier for a person to understand you if you use words indicating the use of the same perception system as he has. And, accordingly, it will be easier for you to penetrate into his inner world and hear just what he had in mind, and not what might have seemed at first glance.

Truisms

A truism is a statement that is easy for the listener to agree with. Because it is either truthful or banal. In any case, if the interlocutor is convinced over and over again that your words are right, your credit of trust is growing in his eyes. And this is just what we need, is not it?

Therefore, we structure our speech so that all our statements turn out to be truisms. How this is done, you will learn a little later. Now, it's important to learn the basic principle: first, they check you, then they trust you. Therefore, we first consent and form the image of a person whose words can be trusted, and then we use it—by inertia.

Inertia

Most people are slaves to habits. Their main desire is for comfort. And comfort is when nothing changes. Therefore, they do not want to change anything. Not in their head. Not in reality. Accordingly, if you can initially set the stereotypes of your communication in the spirit you need, then everything will go like clockwork. By inertia. They already trust you. You are already considered a nice guy. You are already in good standing.

On the other hand, if from the very beginning communication went along an undesirable path, returning to the right track will require more experience in manipulation and additional time that a person needs to come to terms with the idea that much will now be different and develop new ones. However, the techniques for creating confusion will help him accelerate.

Status Management

The adjustment has a wonderful property—it creates such a comfortable feeling of warmth, closeness, and mutual understanding that the interlocutor unconsciously seeks to support it. In a sense, we can say that it begins to depend on our reactions.

So, if, after some time of adjustment, you suddenly sharply tune away in several ways at once, the interlocutor will be very confused, and he will need a lot of time to get together again. If you change your behavior gradually and smoothly, you will notice that changes also occur in the other person. Unconsciously trying to maintain the contact, the interlocutor begins to adapt to you! As they say in NLP—conduct.

In dark psychology, a condition in which both interlocutors adapt to each other is called rapport. It is convenient for us in that we adjust ourselves consciously, and the interlocutor unconsciously—and often, forcedly. And this gives us a certain power to lead the person where we need to—by the condition.

In practice, this means that the addition of skills to build rapport and manage our own conditions gives us the opportunity to invoke the desired mood in our interlocutor discreetly —

complimentary, energetic, enthusiastic, aggressive, sad, apathetic—anyone, the one we need right now. Well, the non-verbal guidance of trance, of course, will not be superfluous in our arsenal.

How it's done? First, you fully adapt to the interlocutor, adopting his state. Then, begin to gradually transition to the state that you need—in this case, immersed in a trance-like state. In this case, of course, your breathing will deepen, your muscles will relax, your voice will change, your movements will slow down—you just have to make sure that the unconscious interlocutor has time to make similar changes with his body, slowing down the speed of your changes if necessary.

This was a bit like school experiments in physics when it was necessary to tie a thread to weight and pull. Pull too sharply—the thread will break, and the weight will not budge. You will have to restore contact. Pull it as it should, the weight will obediently move in the direction you need. So the goal, of course, is important, but without rapport, it will not be possible to bring the interlocutor to a given state.

Inertia of Consent

A person is ready to accept no more than 20% of new information. And this means that in order for him to take on faith one of our statements, we must precede him with four reliable ones. Better more. Only then will he begin to gradually relax and trust our words, assuring himself of our competence.

How does it work? First, we cannot be on our guard all the time. Therefore, we conduct only an initial study of the new, and then the watch system goes into standby mode. Something dangerous will sound. It's right there. Therefore, by the way, you need to talk quite carefully.

Secondly, states of agreement and disagreement are different physiological states. And the body needs time to change them. Therefore, we first carefully provoke a state of consent from the interlocutor, and then we use consent "by inertia."

Thirdly, we use special techniques for smoothing speech, allowing thoughts to flow easily and freely, flowing from one statement to another. Already guessed which ones? Unions.

Responsiveness

The main one in communication is the one they obey. He said people did. He hinted—people did. The higher the authority of the main thing, the less time passes from order to execution. The form of the order is not so important. Most often this is a proposal, a request, or just a mention of a need. It is much more important how soon people will be undermined to fulfill the order.

You are joking - they are laughing. You want water - they bring you. You ask for a loan - they give you. You give the order - execute and report on time. You notice that the floor is dirty - they run after a bucket and a rag. Ask for words - around silence and attentive eyes. You start to speak with insight - people get serious.

Do you want people to obey you? The question is not rhetorical. Quite often, it's useful not to advertise that you have power. Then, you can lead from the shadows. However, for this, too, you need to be able to what is described here—to press hidden buttons. But if everything works out well for you, you don't need to read further.

So, the criterion is clear—time to execution. If it tends to infinity, you are not in authority. And you need to either gain this authority or switch to completely implicit techniques—like sowing suggestions or do both like me. If the time to execution is reduced, you are on the right track.

The second criterion is the degree of difficulty. But you can increase the tension of your requests only when everything is fine with you on the first point. However, it will turn out to increase: people succumb to inertia forces. And if they have already begun to obey you, then most likely they will continue to do so—if everything is done right.

Therefore, the main task for us is to create the correct inertia, to disperse in the right direction—and for this, you need to budge, at least. After all, the most difficult thing is to make the person to respond to our request for the first time. Then, he will do it easily—out of habit. In do this, we make the first request such that it was extremely easy to respond to it—and there was no reason for resistance.

What do I need to do? As much as possible to lower the requirements according to both criteria of authority. Let him fulfill our request someday. For example, when he will be comfortable. And let our request be as simple as possible and not requiring any effort.

Examples:

- Let him look out the window

- Greetings in response to your greeting

- Nods in agreement

- Answers a simple question

- The coat will hang where you tell

- Sits closer

Ask for what he would have done. Tell him how your opinion is more convenient. Launch social stereotypes like a greeting ritual. Use natural reactions. The main thing is that his actions are a response to your words. You said he did. They said—done. They said—done. So the reflex worked out.

And to make it pleasant to obey, you draw up your orders as care and tips. Polite and unobtrusive. You just talk about the possibilities without insisting on anything.

Examples:

- *You will be more comfortable in this chair to take a look at the chart.*

- *This is an important point, it is better to highlight it in red, here is the pen.*

- *If it is not clear, you can ask a question.*

- *So that we can choose the best option for you, please tell us about yourself.*

- *It is useful to write down.*

- *What is the best way to contact you?*

What to do if, despite all your tricks, a person still does not do what is needed? If his expression is neutral, nothing. You prompted; he made a decision. Everything is fine. Just next time, offer action from another realm. He didn't want to write down; maybe he would want to look at the chart. You can, however, say that you do not insist on anything and he is free to do as he knows.

If a shadow of discontent flashed on the face of the interlocutor, it was time to take a step back. Apologize for excessive care, sprinkle ashes on the head, etc. People then thaw.

What gives us the right to continue to work? That is, our proposals should sound less often, their essence is simpler and less stressful, and the subtext behind them is more profitable. In a word, we retreat to previously occupied lines—to come back later.

Examples:

- *Please wash the dishes while I clean the potatoes.*

- *You can begin to implement my recommendations, but for now, I'll think about what else you can tell.*

- *Read the printout of the basic version of the contract while I enter your data into the computer.*

Well, if everything goes like clockwork: the interlocutor does just what we offer, and the time to execution is reduced, you can gradually move on to more serious proposals. More difficult tasks. More costs. More important deadlines. That is just what we started the whole fuss for the sake of. By this time, the person will already get used to the fact that they need to obey, and you are the main one. Even if you consciously do not admit it to yourself. So what? If it is necessary, make it recognized. But usually, this is already superfluous.

Chapter 5:
Consent

I can always make the interlocutor agree with me. However, now, you can say that you personally could argue with me. Yes, at least, right now! True? Well, nice—we still have nothing to share, but this magical book in your hands.

Basic Principle

"The text should flow by itself without catching the listener anywhere. Only then will the words gain magical power."

Let's start "from the opposite." The easiest way to run into an argument is to offend the interlocutor. Trampling on his sense of self-worth is to humiliate. Give a categorical statement that contradicts the convictions he has suffered—to challenge his words. Offer to sacrifice his principles. The menu here is rich!

Accordingly, what? Right! Our task is to be attentive to the interlocutor, to notice the slightest signs of his displeasure and to "move out in the market," "roll back to previously occupied lines" in time.

My husband comes home from work, not only is he late, but he also did not get me anything. The wife sits angry, despising: "You bastard, where did you hang around until nightfall?!"

The husband silently reaches into his pocket, pulls out a wallet full of money. The wife is changing in the face: "Oh, you poor thing, you've completely earned it!" And what do we have on the cheeks? Let me wipe you off!

We start the conversation with the things of strangers. From what was "long and far." Or "not at all with us." And even at all - "read in the newspaper." The less immediate danger in our words, the easier it is for a person to take off his defense. That's good.

At the same time, you need to be ready at any time to answer a dumb question: "And the hell should I listen to this?" The answer is always the same: for his own good. For it is interesting, or useful, or cool, or joyful—think up in advance.

The main thing is that we will gradually approach the essence, starting from afar—but not just approaching, but gaining agreement. After all, when you said "yes" 99 times, it's much easier to say the same thing for the hundredth time. Yes? This is sometimes referred to as inertia consent—sometimes, by building a sequence of acceptance. The essence of this does not change.

We Speak Truisms

So, we learn to speak in such a way that nothing in our words makes the interlocutor alert, and even better, so that he agrees with us over and over again. There are a number of fairly simple tools for this, which we will learn to use right now.

Some tools are:

- Data

- Paraphrase of Recent Replicas

- Citing Beliefs

- Opportunity

- "A" or Not "A"

- Condition

- Proverbs, Sayings, Aphorisms

- About Me

Data

You very easily earn the trust of the interlocutor, if he can quickly see the justice of every word you say. How to provide this? You guessed it: you need to tell the truth about what is easy to verify. And it is very easy. Make sure?

- *Do you want to live well? - Who wants to live poorly does not exist.*

You have already seen that I can come up with at least one verifiable phrases. It remains to learn the same thing for you— such a pun. And that, too, is true.

In fact, being close to a person, it is very easy to come up with non-trivial verifiable theses. After all, do we know what his name is? But can we notice whether he is listening to us or not? Can we speak out about the weather or the situation around? Can we clarify what we have already agreed on? And we can refer to the event, both of which were witnesses. In short, keep your eyes open, and oceans of opportunity will open before you. At least there's no reason to argue with you, right?

A popular sign: "If you had triplets, then two at least two of them are of the same sex."

Paraphrase of Recent Replicas

Paraphrase—a verbatim quotation of the interlocutor with interrogative intonation—is practically a win-win way to obtain the consent of the interlocutor. It is also called the "echo." I remind you that the first task is to transfer a person from a debater to a state of consent. The canonical phrase: "Did I understand you correctly that (literally repeat his words)?"

Of course, a canonical introduction is not necessary. There are others:

- That is

- You meant

- (just interrogative intonation)

- Let me clarify

- So

- Do you think that

Examples:

- *A good car cannot cost less than five thousand euros. - You said "cheaper than five thousand euros"?*

- *I'm not going to report to anyone! - Did I correctly understand that you are not going to report to anyone?*

- *Yesterday I watched a complete masterpiece movie! - A masterpiece movie?*

Citation of Beliefs

Whom do people think are reasonable? Right! Like yourself. More precisely, those who understand them. More precisely, those who agree with them. Up to citation. Accordingly, having learned to agree with the interlocutor and from time to time to return his own maxims to him, we automatically fall into the category of reasonable people. And this is fair.

So why do you need to "keep your ears on top of your head"? Right! It's to earn a credit of trust from the interlocutor. After all, "such an intelligent person cannot speak complete nonsense." We will not. Who is arguing with himself?!

Opportunity

Has it ever happened to you that almost every phrase of the interlocutor invariably evoked your consent? Have you ever met people (at least in a book or a movie) who even managed to broadcast elementary truths in such a way that they wanted to challenge them? Can you recall the case when, on the same occasion, there were arguments for and against?

It seems that there will be a lot of people who will answer "yes" to each question in the previous paragraph. And that is understandable. The world is multifaceted, and what is there just so! Sometimes, mutually exclusive things coexist quite peacefully, not only in its different parts but also in the same person.

Each of us, in some ways, is cowardly; sometimes funny, sometimes sad; hardworking like a bee, lazy like a hundred logs; practical, dreamy; generous or greedy; bright or inconspicuous—at least, sometimes. Each has it all.

Hence, any phrase referring to the single presence of anything was doomed to some commonplace—I mean, indisputability. Does it happen? It happens. Can it? It can. Sometimes, it does in some circumstances—or often, in most cases. Obviously? Fact.

Examples:

- *There probably is a person in your life who has influenced your worldview quite strongly.*

- *It is possible that if you wish, you can easily find what you can agree with me.*

- *Perhaps at some points in your life, you could have done more if you already knew these techniques.*

- *I'm sure you could teach me a lot.*

"A" or Not "A"

The funny thing is that a dispute with yourself is one of the easiest ways to get the guaranteed consent of the interlocutor. However, there is an easier way. If you use the direct statement and the opposite in the same phrase, the phrase will become identically true. By truism that is.

Do you want an example? You can listen to me or not listen. And listening to me, agree with me or disagree. And it really makes sense, because I can tell the truth, but I cannot tell the truth. Do you understand? Each of my phrases is the ultimate truth, though with much desire, each of my phrases can be challenged. It would be a desire.

Examples:

- *Each person can enjoy experimenting with new ideas for him, although, of course, not all.*

- *It seems to me that you are ready to agree with me on everything. Or not in everything?*

- *All women love sex more than men, though not all.*

Condition

A phrase containing an additional condition becomes absolutely true. Of course, provided that you have made it relatively relative, i.e., set the right conditions.

And what are the correct conditions? If they cannot be verified right now, all is well. What other conditions can be set? Independent of the interlocutor. For example, an employer can tell an employee that if he is satisfied with his zeal, good prospects await him. And everything is fair—if you do not take into account the fact that the very structure of such a promise is crafty. Go check what the other has in mind!

Examples:

- *Our company is liked by literally everyone who has not yet been bribed by our competitors.*

- *Fitness classes perfectly heal the whole body if you exercise under the supervision of an experienced instructor with a medical background.*

- *Food can be stored for years if you are not going to eat it.*

- *And the mosquito will fight the horse if the bear helps.*

An additional convenience of the last two types of truism—they allow you to turn off the topic in time if you notice the slightest signs of disagreement with the listener.

Some preachers on the street stuck to a friend. Say: "Do you believe in God?" He replies: "Yes, of course, I believe. I am a Satanist." The preacher is almost hysterical: "How is it that you will go to hell!!" To which he, without a shadow of a doubt, replies: "We will all be in hell, but only I will be there with the pitchfork!"

Proverbs, Sayings, Aphorisms

The power of habits cannot be underestimated. If a person has heard something many times, he is unlikely to argue with this, even if the statement is, to say the least, controversial. Because I'm used to it. Therefore, it's quite safe to quote folk or author's, but long and firmly included utterances. Because "Do not teach your father—and that's great!"

In addition, people (not always consciously) value the beauty of a statement to the detriment of its provability. Therefore, proverbs, sayings, and aphorisms would be greatly lost in "certainty," if some wise guy would have thought to retell them in his own words.

Examples:

- *Without labor, you can't even get fish out of the pond.*

- *No matter how much the wolf feeds, he looks into the forest.*

- *An eye for an eye; a tooth for a tooth.*

About Myself

In everyday life, in communication, and on the couch, which replaced the bed in my house, a squatter (Peter) was clinically mediocre. He considered himself a very ambiguous personality, and this conviction was so strong that it was projected outward, starting to act on me in a hypnotic way during our network communication.

It seems to me that for the first part you have already mastered the subject well. In general, my experience suggests that it is better to be good at one technique than bad at many. And I'm used to trusting my experience. And I feel that is right. Of course, I realize that I continue to demonstrate more and more new types of truisms, but I do not know if the reader notices this. So what: I'm already used to doing my job well, not relying on the active, conscious participation of the other side.

Examples:

- *Near you, I feel safe and can relax.*

- *Personally, I really like this model of vacuum cleaners.*

- *I usually manage to speak convincingly.*

- *People say that my books are easy to read, and it seems to me that they are right.*

In any case, take it for granted: when you talk about yourself, your thoughts and feelings, about your experience, the other person just does not have a chance to challenge you. It seems to me—and you?

Uncertainty

There is a practically guaranteed way to talk so that people cannot argue with you. Its essence is extremely simple—to speak a lot, to speak in such a way that everyone sees something different behind your words, but does not say anything essentially.

Remember the old joke?

"Who is it jumping in the distance?"

- This is the elusive Joe!

"Can no one catch him?"

- No, nobody just needs it for anything.

When you speak accurately enough, when your speech is built fairly technologically, i.e., as I propose doing in this chapter, there is no desire to argue with you. Because "What is there to argue with?" And that's good.

Because we gradually, on these very commonplace, teach a person to nod to us. Agree. And even "politely do not listen." Continuing to agree! And then we have a chance to begin to speak more and more definitely. Everything is more categorical. Closer to the main thing, for the sake of which the whole fuss was started.

But you already know: at the slightest sign of disagreement, we "back up" and again speak more and more blurry. Or more and more verifiable. Or quote the interlocutor himself. And with might and main, we affirm that it is not at all necessary to agree with us. In a word, if the specified condition is met, then you just do not have a chance to fail.

The Illusion of Understanding

What do the words "get me right" mean? How should they understand us so that mutual understanding is complete? You see, understanding between people is impossible in principle—

only the illusion of understanding is possible. I pronounce the words "school, 9th grade," and many of you represent your school and your ninth grade. And quite respectable people can generally imagine their child's school and ninth grade. And teachers—so generally their own. But I had in mind my school and my ninth grade! I say the words "first love," and your imagination rushed in its direction. I mention "good weather," and even that is different. And for some of you, this phrase has caused a steady association with the training of the NLP practitioner course. Well, you have no chance to understand me. Do you understand?

People have no chance to understand each other, but nevertheless, we communicate. And even somehow we manage to do joint business. Maybe this is the secret? I think so—the meaning of communication in the resulting reaction. If as a result of your words, a person has done what you need, he understood you correctly. If not, it's wrong. Moreover, when people really begin to understand what we had in mind, they often stop doing what we need. You understand: "Your commission from the sale will be as much as 3 percent!" Read: "97 percent is mine."

"Understand me correctly," in fact, stands for "Do as I want," and for this, I will do everything so that you do not understand me. Well, you understand.

In order to get the necessary reactions from a person, one must clearly realize that when we pronounce words, we do not operate with our mental images, but with him. And we can track the correct understanding only by observing how a person perceives our speech. In a word, be careful—watch the reaction.

Uncertainty Patterns

To be honest, uncertainty is not good at all but rather definite. Otherwise, there will be a risk that you will just chat pleasantly and the person you are talking to will do what comes to his mind, and not what you want from him. The instructions should be clear and the rationale universal.

How to achieve this? The creators of NLP introduced certainty into this question, bringing Milton Erickson's vague recommendations into precise uncertainty patterns. So you have already been taken care of—just use it.

Uncertainty templates include:

- Non-reference

- Undefined names

- Indefinite verbs

- Estimates

- Nominalization

No Mention

Let me remind you, our task is to say so that a person does what we need. If some information can damage this, we omit it.

For example, at one time I worked for a certain office (I won't call her, so as not to give her free advertising), so during the interview we agreed on the amount of the salary, but the employer did not mention that there is no such thing as a salary day, and employees have money receive when they appear on a new month. By the way, at that time, he did not have money for my payment. And if I knew about this in advance?

I remind you, by the way, we are now talking about the tool, and not about the ethics of its use. Ethics is a matter of setting an ethical goal, and we have a book about a means to an end.

Here's another example. I am hired from time to time to brainwash company employees under the guise of business training. Of course, I do not mention that I myself do not believe in those high ideals and standards that I transmit to them. As a result, people believe.

Here's the third example. The girl in the first trimester settles in the office, where "everything is according to the Labor Code." Question: Will her chances of finding a job increase if she says she is pregnant?

Or so. Yesterday I was in this cafe—the potatoes were over dried, the meat was undercooked. And we will not say that everything was in order with the rest of the food. We let our interlocutor summarize the information that we provided him.

Undefined Names

We already know that. There is always some freedom in choosing the degree of uncertainty. You can say "the chair you are sitting on," or you can say "the chair in this room," or you can say "the chair." You can say "breakfast," you can say "food." You can say, "Natalie Stewarts," or you can just "her."

Agree, if you say "You are often mistaken," many will want to argue with this. But the wording "People often make mistakes" can only cause yawning with its banality.

In general, there is a fairly simple way to find out what a person is actually telling us—to ask the question: "What is he getting from me? What actions?" Then, a lot of things become clear. In particular, it is quite possible not to listen to your ten-minute speech — it all comes down to one phrase: "Give me money."

Indefinite Verbs

With verbs—the same song, but only more interesting. I can easily show you this, but you yourself can find suitable examples—you just have to try and give your own imagination a little work.

- Change position

- Spread your legs

- Get up

- Pull out

- To the left

- To the right

- Above

- Below

- Good

- Do not rush

You can ask a person to help, and when he agrees, it turns out that financial help is needed—or the piano on the seventh floor without an elevator needs to be dragged, or deal with bandits.

You can tell how you were humiliated by your boss, who behaved rudely and underestimated you.

You can complain that you have nothing to go out into the world and you are afraid to disgrace yourself in front of respected people.

A woman at the dentist's appointment lies in an armchair—her mouth is frozen, and the doctor carefully drills something. Then, the patient's cell phone begins to burst. After the fifth call, the doctor doesn't stand it and grabs the phone furiously:

"Hey!!!"

- Hey!!! - also a male voice. Doctor:

"Who are you??!!!"

- HUSBAND!!!

"Listen, husband; I'll finish now—she will spit, and she'll call you back!!!"

The verb is not specific by definition, as it is intended to reflect the process. And the process is something that is time-stretched, which means it does not exist at any given moment. But this is metaphysics.

Grades

This is a very good and effective tool. With its help, you can achieve amazing results. A remarkable property of estimates is that they do not carry any information at all. There is nothing behind them—i.e., nothing at all.

But what a grandiose influence! Evaluations color our speech with emotions. Estimates allow us to easily and elegantly form the attitude we need, and in a completely arbitrary way!

It's one thing to say "sweet prank," it's quite another to say "vile abomination." It's one thing to qualify the subordinate's lateness as "the competent use of the principles of effective time management," and "a malicious violation of labor discipline, shocking disrespect for one's colleagues and co-workers" will sound completely different.

"What is rum?"

- Well, it's such a pirate vodka.

"Ah, got it! Unlicensed."

Nominations

There is a simple check for nominalization: can this noun be put in a wheelbarrow? Accordingly, nominalization is a void by definition. Meanwhile, these are the words that most affect our behavior. An essential part of humanity over the centuries has been controlled by just two words: "holy" and "sin." Try it yourself! To drink in the morning is sacred! And stopping this is a sin!

On a criminal law exam:

"Can you tell me what cheating is?"

- *It will happen, professor, if you fail me.*

"How? Explain."

- *According to the Criminal Code, deceit is committed by one who, using the ignorance of another person, causes damage to that person.*

There are a lot of nominations—and each of them is a bomb. People take links to such words seriously as a real argument.

Examples:

- Corporate culture

- Research results

- Identified patterns

- Regulations

- Punishment

- Company's mission

- Concept ("This is not part of our concept...")

- Experience ("As my experience says...")

- Care ("Let's take care of...")

- Understanding ("I hope for your understanding...")

In my deep conviction, for success in communication, it is quite enough to pay enough attention to the basis of your own argumentation. And this, of course, is nominalization.

Why clean shoes? It's to watch karma. Why should I buy this? Fashionable. Why do I need insurance? For confidence in your future. What is the most expensive? Self-esteem. What is the tip for? For the service. What prevents you from meeting a girl? Complexes. Why is this tree on the windowsill? It's for comfort, and in general, peace in the family. Got it?! In a word, beauty is a terrible force!

Chapter 6:
What We Convince

The Japanese are unsurpassed PR masters, skinny suffocates who did not win a single competition but told the whole world a tale of crushing karate and invincible ninjas—cowardly and timid, and taught the whole world to respect the spirit of the samurai—not able to connect the four lines in a rhyme, but explained to everyone that three lines without rhyme are the greatest of poetry! And how do they sell their cars and electronics? They do so with a bang! Because they explained to everyone: Japanese technology is the best in the world. And now, their food—a clump of unwashed rice with a slice of raw fish on top—and soy soup out of the water!

By and large, colloquial hypnosis has two main goals: building a convenient subjective reality in our interlocutor's head and directly provoking the desired behavior or state.

The inner world of any person consists of his experiences. From what he sees, hears, and feels. Including within itself. Observations, memories, plans, interpretations—and what gives order to this sensory chaos? What turns colored spots into recognizable objects and phenomena? In people, in the rain, in letters on paper? What makes the signal of heat and pressure under the knee of one leg and above the knee of the other a "leg lies on the leg"? The words!

It is the words that filter and form the information flowing through the sensory organs. And if a person does not know the meaning of a word, he will not be able to perceive the phenomenon that it means. Therefore, two people observing the same thing see different things! One sees the "car," the other - "Dodge Viper ACR-X." One sees the "group dynamics," the other - that "Martin is offended." One hears a "subtle harmonic transition," the other a "strong text." The words are different.

Words are a fixative for the experience. Therefore, if a person once accepted for himself a judgment about himself or about the world, he will notice—or even look for it—exclusively that this judgment confirms. "I am successful" forces us to take from the experience all the signs of my success. "It is harmful" does not allow you to see anything that refutes this opinion. "We must stay clear of infectious people" makes us ignore all cases when you have been in contact with carriers of infection and have remained healthy.

That is why suggestions are such an attractive target for manipulation.

Judgments for Behavior

In fact, we have already done all the preparatory work that allows us to use the words in the right way. We already know how to choose the correct (convenient for us) description of reality, we are able to translate the interlocutor into a state of agreement. We have learned to use the effect of an agreement by inertia. We can speak so generalized that the listener is able to bring his own experience adequately under our words.

Perfect! We have all the necessary bricks from which we can begin to build models of the world—to make generalizing judgments. Because just describing reality is not enough—we must learn to make sure that the behavior we need directly follows from our description. And not some other! In this case, the person himself will draw all the conclusions we need, and we can say that "it's not us like that—this is such a life," and leave the person the freedom to make the decision we need independently.

Examples:

- You can suggest: "Fall in love with me!" But it's better to complain aloud that "It's impossible not to fall in love with people of my type."

- You can crush: "Take out the trash!" But it is better to note that "If you do not take out the trash, it will stink all night."

- You can push: "Take on the job!" But it's better to suggest that "luck is only for those who work hard."

In other words, a person will make sense to do what we gently prompt him. As in the famous parable of the workers, the first of which stupidly laid stones in a row, the second made a flat wall, and the third—built a temple. Which of them do you think felt the greatest pleasure of the same work? The question is rhetorical.

Judgment Templates

I suppose you don't have to be too smart to figure out who convinced the population to consider high art that no one on the globe would ever think of acquiring at least a dime. But the mediocrity managed to elevate the level of its worthlessness into a "cult."

As you have already seen, using templates opened by John Grinder and Richard Bandler is quite simple. This removes all the questions regarding "speaking smartly," since it comes to understanding that the interlocutor will fill your templates with his own meaning anyway. And the guarantee that, despite this, you will be understood correctly, i.e., will do what you want is the correct application of colloquial hypnosis patterns.

Judgment templates are as follows:

- Generalizations

- Opportunity operator

- Obligation operator

- Lost author

Generalizations

"Everything," "everything," "everywhere," "any," "everyone," "nobody," "never," "nobody," and so on. It is clear to everyone that not a single bit of meaningful speech can do without these words. Everyone strives to at least something to generalize. Of course, I do not claim that each phrase contains at least one (possibly implicit) generalization, but no one has yet been able to prove the opposite. Perhaps we are all mistaken. People generally do this often, and usually, it does not lead to any fatal consequences.

When we talk about introducing the necessary beliefs into the subjective reality of the interlocutor, we always mean one or another template of judgments. Moreover, it is not so much what we said that is important, but what left its mark. If I say that "I don't know whether it is true that my every statement is useful to you," it's just a generalization that remains in my head. And for any objection, I have insurance: "I said so that I don't know if this is true..." In a word, they threw the right thought and, before conscious control, got bogged down. Conveniently.

More examples of generalizations:

- *A real man is a non-smoker.*

- *Everyone loves mambas! (And the mamba hates all!!!)*

- *Good housewives love gloss.*

- *Never deny friends.*

- *All valuable things must be insured.*

Opportunity Operator

When we say that something can be, we are almost certainly right. Because really—anything happens. At least sometimes. At least someone. And when we say that people can agree with us, we may well be right. After all, there can be at least one person who agrees with us. So, everything is in order. Our words can be confirmed by facts.

In addition, you may notice that the fact does not even have to be accomplished—the potential is quite enough. Can Japan (at least hypothetically) unleash a war with Zimbabwe? Can. May an employee want to rob his company? Yes. You can - imagine! - want to give me all your money? But what about! In theory. And then - "sediment remained."

Here are some keywords:

- I can, you can, maybe

- Perhaps it happens, it happens, exists

- Some, sometimes

Examples:

- You can change shoes here.

  (Change your shoes.)

- This person can fail.

  (Do not deal with him.)

- It is possible that we are the best company in the industry.

  (Collaborate with us.)

Duty Operator

Hence, after we talked for some time with truisms, in the pattern of uncertainty, soft generalizations, and possibilities, we should move on to more serious intervention in the inner world of the interlocutor. Unless, of course, we plan to wait a few years until he deigns to take advantage of the opportunities described by us. Maybe it should! Let it be clear.

Of course, saying all this, it is necessary to constantly monitor a person's reactions in order to be able to recover in time. And since this happened, we will have to use the whole arsenal of neat speech to convince him that he just misunderstood us, and his direct duty is to understand us correctly.

In some sources, the propositional pattern is called the constraint pattern of the world model. We limit the set of possible choices to the one that now has to be made. It's just that the world is such that there is no choice.

Examples:

- A modern person must succeed. To do this, you need to learn a lot, and then work hard. And wait for this a lot of money in the first five years - it is impossible.

- Each employee is required to donate money to the CEO's birthday.

- Every woman needs to have at least five skirts of different lengths.

- Be sure to order sushi.

I cannot help but notice that adding negation to the opportunity operator turns it into a must operator. *"I cannot do otherwise..."*

- I could not miss such a terrific blouse!

- You cannot ignore the laws of logical thinking.

In a word, with all the wealth of choice, there is no other "alternative." And who said that, actually?

Lost Author

Obviously, the enumeration of propositional patterns would not be complete without a description of the pattern called the lost author. Of course, now we will analyze it in sufficient detail. After all, life is arranged in such a way that the absence of a single tool can be fatal for the whole thing.

So, it is well known that the absence of an indication of the authorship of a particular judgment makes it somewhat more certain. You can argue with the author, and when there is no author, with whom to argue? "It's not us like that—it's such a life."

Man is an imperfect being. People tend to make mistakes. And this means that even a genius who has made this or that judgment can be easily challenged. After all, could he be mistaken? Could. But if there is no author, his subjective opinion becomes the truth about the world. In the minds of listeners, of course.

Agree, there is a certain difference between the phrase: "Uncle Paul from the third entrance, being, as usual, drunk, said that everyone could succeed," and the shorter motto, "Everyone can succeed!"

There are authors, the link to which spoils everything—from the perspective of this particular listener. Some are not ready to perceive the truths personally from you; the other will meet with hostility any expression of an unpleasant person; some do not like certain politicians. And if earlier, the reference turned any nonsense into a truism, now they mention it—more carefully. In the same way, as the Bible was often quoted, "forgetting" to refer to it. "Yes must be yes; no must be no."

What usually camouflages a hidden author? Introductory words like:

- Well-known

- Science has proven

- Experiments have shown

- Obviously

- No brainer

- It was found out

It is already obvious to you that these introductory words are the essence of uncertainty patterns. Including non-reference, of course. That is what you already know how to do perfectly.

Chapter 7:
Pseudology

Logic is the science of the laws of right thinking. Its meaning is to give people the opportunity, based on obvious facts and proven patterns, to draw the right conclusions about the non-obvious. Thanks to logic, we do not have to make our own experience that hitting a knife in the heart can kill any of us. The ability to draw a conclusion based on the assertions that "a knife in the heart kills a person" and "I am a person" is quite enough. This is the power of logic.

Another thing is that most people have not studied logic—and most of those who study it rarely apply the requirements to their own lives. But both those and others appreciate "logic." In the spirit of "Sounds logical" - it means true. Therefore, logic is replaced by its phantom - pseudology, using the same speech turns, but already without any serious reason. And since the vast majority of people use it, it is precisely the pseudology we will use to influence this very majority. Is it logical?

From Truisms to Judgments

It happens that the observed facts somehow do not very clearly testify in our favor, but meanwhile, it is precisely the premises that make the conclusions solid. As a result, there is a need for a tool that allows us to throw a bridge from what we have to what we need. Agree, if you, with the grace of a magician, are able to show how it follows from a regular change of day and night that a contract with your company will bring unthinkable benefits to your future customers, your negotiator's capabilities increase just fantastically.

Many people make a big mistake trying to juggle facts, wishful thinking because it's so easy to catch a lie. And after that, there is no faith for them. But they would like a completely different reaction.

I don't know how others do, but we have only three seasons at home:

- "Don't open the window, and it's so hot!"

- "Don't open the window, and it's so cold!"

- "Don't open the window, and it's so normal!"

If you promised the client a rise in stock prices, but it is not there, it's stupid to try to prove that stocks are getting more expensive—base your arguments on what is. That a fall in prices is a sign of a future take-off and, if he buys a few more securities, his profit will increase significantly. Refer to the patterns of the ebb and flow, to the change of seasons, to regroup before the onset. Explain that a big jump is impossible without a good takeaway, and sometimes you need to back off a little to take off. Point out that the price drop may not be coincidental. Rumor has it that major market players are intentionally knocking down prices in order to buy everything later. And so on.

Friends congratulate the lawyer on the fact that he achieved the acquittal of an obvious criminal.

"You were just great!" They shout enthusiastically, interrupting each other.

"Thank you," the celebrity answers. "But if I did not act as a defender, but as a prosecutor, I would certainly send him to the gallows!"

Pseudology Templates

Samaritans consider chickens as dirty animals because they eat worms, and worms eat the dead, which means that he who eats chicken devours his ancestors.

If you carefully read the previous material, you, of course, noticed that pseudology connects different judgments together, making it possible to substantiate less obvious theses with indisputable truisms. And here comes an elegant game with a template of uncertainty and a template of judgments.

The great joy in using these templates is that people tend to check arguments and justifications, but not the connectives that make up the whole essence of pseudology.

Pseudological templates include:

- "And," "A," and "But"

- "Means"

- Temporary ligaments

- Cause-effect

"And," "A," "But"

We already played a little with the unions, when we passed the agreement by inertia, and became convinced of their strength. And now we will bring some variety, and this will add you additional understanding and new nuances of dark psychology.

What have we already played? We turned a sequence of unrelated phrases into a logical chain.

- This book is about dark psychology; you read the text; you understand it; you study; your life is changing.

- This book is about dark psychology, and you read the text and understand it, and you learn, and your life changes.

But what is good for study, is not always good for practice. Such an abundance of the same type of unions cannot but arouse suspicion, and yet our work should be invisible. What to do?

To begin with, let us leave alliances only where they are justified. It turns out:

- This book is about dark psychology, and you read the text and understand it. You study, and your life changes.

Where the connection is most "strained," we put a more appropriate union:

- This book is about dark psychology, and you read the text and understand it. After all, you study, and your life is changing.

Unlike "and," "a" implies not so much a merger as a division, but with the preservation of the illusion of connectedness.

But that is not all. If we want to show not only merging and parallel processes, but also introduce an element of opposition into the discussion, we can use the "but" union.

- It is impossible to say with certainty that Ori-Lai cosmetics conceal female beauty, but I know people who are sure of this.

In particular, we can create a complete illusion of objective reasoning, saying, in fact, the same thing. But, on the other hand, we can say just what we need and increase our influence on the interlocutor, and at that time he will enthusiastically listen to our "dispute," which is not a dispute, but only we know about it, and we use this knowledge to the fullest extent, and this is called, in some sources, chatter, and we call chatter a little different, but more about that another time. Is it logical?

Actually, no, it's not logical—but it does *sound* logical.

The priest in his car stopped in the area of the "Stopping is prohibited" sign.

A traffic cop comes up and says:

"Sorry, Father, but you have sinned."

For example, you want your subordinate to take on a project that requires additional time but is not paid. What can I tell him? Mitchell, you are in good standing with me, and I am very grateful to you for always meeting my requests. I am glad that we work together, and I want to do everything so that you grow and develop here and you would be interested and profitable here. But now doubts are overwhelming me if you can get down to our new project, and I'm not used to doubting such reliable people, but the project is painfully responsible, and your participation in it is useful for you. Yes, and you are a good guy, and as a specialist, you stand out—but probably, you can do it. What do you think?

That would convince me.

- Sorry, young man, you won't tell me what time it is, or my husband is on a business trip, and I turned 23 today, oddly enough, but I laid the table for two, and suddenly forgot what

time the pharmacy works to buy contraceptives but I can do without them.

"So"

You just felt the effectiveness of allied ligaments, which means that you already know how to do the most important thing in pseudology, which means that you only have to figure out the jewelry, which means you can easily do it. Is it logical? As you may have guessed, now we will consider the interpretation of values.

A lawyer appears in court:

- Gentlemen of the jury! The very fact that the accused chose me as his lawyer testifies to his complete insanity.

This is another pseudology template designed to indicate the equivalence of the proposed judgments, which means that you can easily equate any unobvious statement with a truism with which it is a sin to disagree. So, you get one of the most powerful speech tools in your hands. Of course, provided that you can do all the previous things well, that is, you can easily speak with truisms, that is, you have trained a lot and productively before. So, we will train.

Examples:

- *You refuse—that means you don't value my offer and don't respect me—and that means I won't return your debt, either.*

- *I give from the whole heart, which means you can't refuse—therefore, take it.*

- *You have undertaken logistics obligations, which means you had to deal with customs, so cover losses.*

Time Binding

Starting the conversation about time ligaments, I would like to note that time is inexorable and it runs forward all the time. And linking the two processes together using this template, we transfer the properties of one process to another. For example, when one of them ends, something significant should happen to the other. And while you are thinking about this feature, I will give some examples of the use of time-binding.

Examples:

- While you are "pulling the rubber," your competitors are sharing your lost profits.

- You can continue to weigh the pros and cons while experimenting with trial lots.

- While your colleagues are correcting the mistakes you have made, you cannot take an elementary step towards them.

- Over the years, you begin to understand that you need to get pleasure right now, but it is already too late.

- And as I lay out my arguments one by one, you more clearly understand that there just is no other way.

- After you make the right decision, we can talk about further development prospects.

People often make the mistake of believing that "after" means "due to," that is, imposing causal relationships on temporary ones. Understanding clearly that this is in our hands, we nevertheless distinguish cause-effect ligaments into a separate category.

Cause-Effect

A causal relationship is the most arrogant way to combine judgments since it involves the most stringent mutual coupling between events. Therefore, we begin to use coercive ties only when the interlocutor, without wincing, swallows all our limitations of his model of the world, not to mention the truisms. And if so, we should be especially attentive to the slightest signs of displeasure on the face of the listener, in which case, turn into a side street.

The store owner watches as a young seller does service the buyer:

"Since you pick up the hooks, why don't you pick up the fishing line?"

- Well, give a couple of coils.

"But a new spinning is needed for such a good fishing line!"

- Perhaps you are right.

"What about the net? You can't do without it."

- Well, let's get the net."

"And how do you enter the water without marsh boots?"

- Okay, I'm taking my boots, too!

When the buyer, having paid, leaves, the owner turns to the seller:

"How did you manage to persuade the buyer who came for the hooks?"

- Yes, he didn't come by for hooks. He thought that we had a pharmacy and came for tampons—his wife had monthly periods—but I explained to him that there was nothing to do at home for several days and advised him to go fishing.

Examples:

- *You have honest eyes, so I can be honest with you.*

- *I love you, so we must be together.*

- *The sight of someone else's suffering in any normal person causes a desire to help.*

- *Walking through the forest is completely safe because in the winter the bears hibernate.*

- *You would have earned a round sum this month, but for some reason, you did not seek our advice on time.*

- *We found out that you need reliable household appliances, so I gave all the necessary evidence of the reliability of our vacuum cleaner, and since I was able to do this, you must either indicate what other reasons you need or make a purchase right now, because the system of instant discounts is valid only until tomorrow.*

What gives us the right to such conclusions? A simple feature of human communication: our language is so vague and illogical in itself that we cannot physically verify the logic of each utterance. And if we take it seriously, we will have to find fault with each replica of each interlocutor. Why do we need a reputation for being boring?

What is the main thing for us? The fact that most of our interlocutors are used to trusting speech that sounds logical. And if you didn't say something really rude, they will quite peacefully accept everything that you offer them, checking from time to time the justification of your judgments. Therefore, make sure that the judgment after the union "because" is a truism, as well as the judgment before the "therefore." There are enough people to check the initial premises, but few will undertake to check the links themselves. That's why we are in force.

Chapter 8:
Subtleties — How to Use Manipulation for Empathic Relationships, Friendship, and at Work

I want to inspire—I know, teach me how! This is a typical manipulation and dark psychology learning request. It is easy to satisfy. You come to the trainer, he teaches you how to make trance and how to formulate indirect suggestions, and in the lessons, you already succeed—but when you notice that the interlocutor "swam" and you could give him a command, it often turns out that in order to inspire, there is nothing. Own thoughts run-up, but there are no normal working templates yet. And that's all—the moment is lost.

There are two reasons for this. First: you just don't know what you want. Do not know your desires. In a milder version: you do not know what to want from this particular interlocutor. The cure is simple: sit down and write a list of your desires. When there are many desires, it is easy to see the possibilities for realizing at least one of them. Further: before the meeting, consider why you are going to it, what you would like to receive from this person. And imagine the result as a picture. Usually, it makes sense to instill either the right behavior or the right attitude towards something. On that and we will solve.

The second reason: you are afraid that upon hearing your suggestion, the interlocutor will come out of the trance and give you in the face. Well, or make a claim in any other form. Well, practice shows that these fears are justified, and an inexperienced person can really run into. If it inspires not something and not what wakes up the internal watchman of his "victim." What suggestions are safe, we will analyze further.

Courtesy Rules

It is helpful to treat suggestions as polite requests. Indeed, it is much more pleasant instead of "Look at the clock and tell me what time it is!" To hear the indirect "Can you tell me the time?" Or "Do you have a watch?" De facto, these are indirect suggestions. Manipulation. But they are perceived by requests.

A request is nicer than a demand. Requests are polite. And everyone knows from childhood that if you are asked politely, it is already impolite to refuse. Therefore, politeness is almost the most effective form of suggestion. But after all, to be honest, I don't want to fulfill all the requests? *Could you dance at the table of your boss?" "Please give me all your money!" "Won't it bother you to surrender to me tonight?" - Not everyone is ready to fulfill such wishes. What's the secret?*

A person will gladly fulfill our request if three conditions are met:

- He understands what needs to be done. He knows how to do it.

- It is easy and stress-free for him. Do not have to spend too much and strain.

- It seems to him that fulfilling the request is beneficial to him.

If at least one of these conditions is violated, you can at least get out of touch; he will not do it soon—then *when* the conditions change.

Two men are walking along the street. One, as it were, incidentally says to the other:

"I am the strongest telepath and generally inspire from a distance..."

- Yah you!

"Look, now the TV is thrown out of that balcony."

He stared at the balcony. A man ran out and threw down the TV.

- Well, how?

"Well, you, all this is by accident. You try to flatter it again—but hey, that apartment. It will be far away and even higher. So let's check."

- Well, look.

He looked that way bizarrely.

No results.

The telepath tensed, his eyes bulged.

No results.

The telepath grunted and crouched with tension.

The door opens on the balcony; a man runs out:

"Well, I have NO TV!!!"

Do you want another example? Suppose we need to be brought home. If we turn to an experienced driver (1st condition), who is on the road (2nd condition), and he expects to enjoy communication on the road or in return service in the future (3rd condition), then we will be taken without question.

If he does not know the city, or he still needs to go somewhere behind the car or smells bad to us, we will go on foot.

In a word, to be polite, it is not enough to learn the words "please" and "thank you," you still need to keep track of your requests to meet the three conditions of courtesy: comprehensibility, tension, and profitability for the interlocutor. Then, everything will be fine.

A Reminder

I remind you that our task is to speak in such a way as to dull the vigilance of the interlocutor, and not at all the other way around. What does the sentinel system of any living creature respond to? Right! A sharp and unmotivated change in the situation. If you walk along the street and suddenly even smiling and decently dressed people begin to approach you quickly, the subconscious will sound the alarm and throw a portion of adrenaline into the blood—for a fight or for flight. If you are talking peacefully with a person, and he suddenly begins to speak twice as loud (quieter, faster, higher), you understand that something is wrong and you need to beware.

But we are not just living beings—we are thinking beings. We have beliefs, principles, attitudes. And all this we are ready to protect more than our own body. Therefore, in order to dull the vigilance of the interlocutor, you need to say something that is consistent with his ideas about reality. It happens. So it is necessary. That's right. Do you want to agree with this?

All the same, a person will not do what is contrary to his beliefs. So do not offer this! It would be strange if you suggested a person take poison and he would gladly agree. Do you agree? But to take medicine is welcome. It would be strange if people gave money just like that, but for bracelets charged with healing prana, they very much give.

If you believe in the healing properties of these bracelets, it's rare that anyone is ready to give orders to experience excitement, but to listen to someone else's exciting experience is welcome—or at least, about love at first sight.

When you inspire, make sure that your words are consistent with the beliefs of the interlocutor. With you knowing the logic, it is easy to choose safe-sounding messages from which the correct behavioral conclusions will flow logically—out of the competence of a consultant is the need for a large fee, out of the danger of influenza is the need to pay for the vaccine, out of the importance of the project is the need to work overtime. Inspire the promises—the person will accept the conclusions.

Inspired Mood

It is difficult to describe the whole gamut of feelings that overwhelmed me at that moment. Here was the delight of access to the great sacrament, and the thrill of its truly universal scope, and the sweet, languid foreboding of inevitable work—quite familiar in essence, but unprecedented in scope. Something like this for American tourists visiting the ruins of the Colosseum.

Most of our decisions are made under mood pressure. Conscious or not. I like this man—I take him to work. The specialist is good, but causes irritation—I do not take it. The Christmas tree toy is ugly but happy. The car is expensive, but awkward. Emotions dominate! If a person does not like his decision, he will find a way to change it, and he will figure out how to justify it—extremely logical!

We live in a world where everyone thinks that logic is at the forefront. In sales training, we are taught to select logical arguments. At negotiations training, we are taught to build reinforced concrete logic. Relations and those are disassembled using the scalpel of logical thinking. Thoughts are put at the forefront, and therefore, the influence through emotions gives fantastic results!

Why would you think that the vast majority of women outstrip such smart men in relationships with amazing ease? They just have not lost touch with their feelings—and they can play on this field, where men forgot how to play way back in childhood.

People do not take the emotional impact seriously and therefore cannot resist it. A person is generally not able to consciously resist what he does not know about its existence—which means that inspiring emotions is both effective and safe, which is required. How to inspire, you know: to infect with mood plus, of course, to colorize speech with emotional words. "Yesterday I watched such a cool movie! Just wow! I've got goosebumps!!!" However, anchoring also works.

Compliments

Few people immediately agree to consider you above yourself. The suggestion, "I am more important!" is dangerous if not confirmed by official instructions. And then, few will allow you to evaluate yourself out loud. And the suggestion, "Listen to my opinion!" also rarely works—but there is one loophole that you know about. Right! Compliments!

A compliment is the type of assessment that is accepted. This is polite. Yes, and nice, to be honest. I just want to believe them—especially if there is a reason. "Great job!" "Amazing hairstyle!" "Fine move!" "Next to you, I'm like a stone wall!" But agreeing to accept compliments, people agree with everything else—that the opinion of the evaluator is important—what rights does he have to evaluate what is more important? After all, he who evaluates is more important, right? Well, you do not dare to tell the boss that he is doing a good job.

Compliments are socially acceptable and, therefore, safe—unless, of course, speak them in moderation. And for this, there are special tricks.

And, saying compliments, we teach a person to accept our suggestions. But they are not so simple—if you look closely. Indeed, a positive assessment is also a requirement of conformity.

You are kind - be kind. You are generous - do not be greedy. You are brave - protect me. You are caring - help bring the bag. You are talented - think for yourself. You are charismatic - charge the team with energy. You are punctual - come on time. Match in a new word for your needs.

By the way, it is often enough to just reduce the intensity of praise relative to the usual level so that the person realizes that he has done something wrong. Women know. But this is another song.

Only PR

On the one hand, praising yourself, your goods, your services are not accepted. On the other hand, you won't surprise anyone. This is normal. The only thing that is important to monitor here is the relevance of the statements. They should be on the subject. It would be strange on a romantic date to start praising the furniture of our own production.

If you have a good reason to say good things about yourself, act! Show yourself from the best sides! Show off more. These are suggestions! After a certain number of repetitions, a person will just get used to thinking about you just as you tell about yourself. "I did a successful project." "I caught a cool combination." "The boss said that I am a very valuable specialist." "It's strange, but for some reason, women like me." "I will be pleased if you think well of me." True, good examples?

Does the man praise you? Thank and do not forget to mention that he is not the only one who thinks so. All honest people adhere to just such an opinion about you. For example, say that his review will be the pearl of your collection of positive reviews about your work. It is actually the same. Awards, diplomas, won contests, titles—why don't people find out about them? They form your reputation!

And if I do not like to brag? Then, praise yourself indirectly. "Yesterday a friend called whom I often help out, he told me…" "A week ago, at a festival dedicated to awarding our company, I saw a girl in a stunning dress! I want this too!" "When my friend, the head of the cosmetology clinic, and I went to Cyprus…" The most important thing is in relative clauses.

Since self-praise is the same suggestion—all speech strategies of indirect suggestions work here. Praise yourself sweetly and charmingly, and people will forgive your easy boasting—but the positive charge remains. It's a fact.

Total Correct suggestions are those on which one is not ashamed to be caught. These are suggestions that are easy to accept, and the actions arising from them are relaxed and subjectively beneficial. This effect is achieved by the fact that we say only that which is consistent with the interlocutor's ideas about reality, and that from which the behavioral consequences are not obvious—about the mood, about attitude, about the qualities, about me—or just ask about what a person would gladly agree to himself. Well, fine.

Chapter 9:
Leverage – Use Emotions and Other Nuances

Some negotiations determine your life for months and years to come, and the price is huge. The example closest to the people is negotiations on salary. I agreed to a salary of a hundred dollars less—feel free to multiply this hundred by 6, 12, 24—depending on how soon you will be able to win it back. All this is a loss from just meeting—sometimes, a second of weakness—but once struck the right to a free work schedule, and you can use it until the dismissal.

But this is, by and large, pennies! After all, there are meetings at which destinies of far greater sums, services, terms, conditions, etc. are decided. And the price of an error on them is enormous— as well as winning in the case of the desired outcome. Therefore, it makes sense to prepare—to win.

What Determines the Outcome of Negotiations?

"I called him, said, well, why do you need this tender? Everything is ready for us—the name is excellent, the package of documents is ready, we conducted a focus group,

and it was a fantastic sensation. We are ready to give it all to you, but it will cost extra money. Twelve thousand."

- And did he believe you, Daniel?" - Sasha squinted incredulously.

"You must be able to talk to such people—tone, politeness, unwavering, and arguments."

- Arguments?

This is how our world works.

I do not undertake to list all the factors. I can't even guarantee that I will describe the main ones. I'll give a list based on what the participants of my training said. For convenience, I will divide it into two: internal and external factors. The inner ones depend on you to a greater extent—external, to a lesser extent, indirectly.

The internal factors include:

- Availability and quality of purpose

- An extensive negotiation plan

- Communication skills

- Availability and quality of information about yourself, the interlocutor, the subject of negotiations

- Internal attitudes, expectations, attitude towards the future

- Emotional condition

- The physical state

- Pain points, weaknesses, fears, doubts

- Stereotype, stereotyped behavior, and reactions

The external factors include:

- Internal factors of the opponent

- Availability and quality of alternatives to negotiations

- The situation, witnesses to the negotiations

- Third parties influencing contracting parties

- Availability of a reserve of time, time for negotiations

- Market, political, cultural, etc. situation

- Laws, concepts, customs, rules

As you can see, the lists are wide enough to bring real benefits to future negotiations—unless, of course, they serve as the basis for real action—but that is up to you.

Need to Prepare!

The best impromptu is homework. It doesn't matter who the first to say so. This is folk wisdom. Rehearsal is the key to success—and if an experienced negotiator can't afford to be unprepared, then for us, it is an impermissible luxury.

Or you need to come to terms with a possible defeat immediately.

Goal to Be

Without a goal, there is no success. Without a goal, there is no reason. Without a goal, there is no effective criterion for evaluating one's actions. The goal should be! The goal focuses on the effort. The target allows you to cut off the excess. The target does not allow you to be manipulated. The goal is a guideline at any point in the negotiations. A goal is a reference point.

If you do not have a goal, set it—or do nothing.

Set the Target Correctly

A true goal gives strength, excitement, and joy—incorrect—immerses in fog, doubt, and longing. The goal must be set correctly, such as this:

- The purpose of communication is the desired behavior of the interlocutor. Where should he nod? What should he agree with? What should he do? What should he stop doing? What should he say? Imagine achieving your goal in the form of an imaginary film. Clear and specific.

- The purpose of communication should be meaningful. The meaning is in approaching the fulfillment of some kind of desire. What do you come close to achieving your goal? To the car, to fame, to love, to power, to relaxing at the resort, to a new suit? What is your wish coming true soon? Imagine too. Desire should please you. Heartily.

I want to work for such a goal. This goal is understandable; it gives clarity. Set the target correctly.

Do You Have a Plan?

It should be. If you have a plan, you know what to do next. You see further. You think better. You know what to do *if* something happens. You have a margin of safety. And that makes you calmer and more confident—if the plan is thought out, or if you have worked through all the options more than once or twice, or if you rehearsed.

The plan should be:

- Complete - Your actions cover all the conditions necessary to achieve the goal.

- Multivariate - The most likely reactions of the interlocutor are provided. There is an option for unforeseen reactions.

- Based on the knowledge of the situation, psychology, oneself, and the interlocutor, it should also be mastered and rehearsed in all cases. Then, everything is simple.

Learn to Communicate

Communication mastery is made up of a whole palette of skills. Offhand:

- Ability to establish and maintain contact with the interlocutor, inspire subconscious trust

- Ability to speak convincingly, coherently, *logically*

- Ability to ask questions, manage the course of the conversation

- Ability to induce conversational trance and use it

- Ability to speak is interesting and long

- Ability to instill the necessary information, attitude, and actions

- Ability to "walk" on the topics of conversation

- Ability to create the right atmosphere

- Ability to find compelling arguments for the interlocutor

- Ability to track involuntary reactions of the interlocutor and to build their behavior based on the feedback received

- Ability to change the interlocutor's attitude to events and phenomena

- Ability to listen to the interlocutor and find common ground

- *And so on*

All of this needs to be studied, studied, and studied again—as bequeathed to the leader of the working people—and you will also be satisfied.

Information Is Everything!

If you know that he will be "fired up" in the event of a breakdown in negotiations, or if you have facts proving his betrayal to his wife, or if you are sure that he dreams of tickets to the nearby Concert Hall—negotiations are easier, right?

If you do not know that the product you are buying is defective— if you do not know that most of the interlocutor's arguments are falsified, or if you do not realize that he is ready for big concessions—you risk losing, even if you think you won.

Gather information! Look for the information! Buy information! Analytical market reviews. Specialized information portals. Corporate website. Personal website of the opponent. Articles, memoirs. Former colleagues, classmates, neighbors, relatives. Well-wishers and detractors. Information—the sea! Just dig in.

Tune in to Success

We constantly program ourselves. The only question is whether to win or to lose. I often say: no matter what a person thinks about himself, he is always right. He considers himself a failure—he is waiting for break-ins and disappointments, and he considers himself a successful person.

The first step to success is to dare to set a strong goal—request a lot. The second step is to convince yourself that you deserve it. And if the slightest doubt arises, repeat to yourself: "I can!" The third point: think of any mental options for events to the desired result.

Life Is a Game!

A good installation for negotiations is installation for the game. Game attitude. Who will replay whom? As a rule, serious negotiators lose to players: they cannot withstand stress. And the players are relaxed, they get high from the process itself. And they win. Play! In the end, what is our life?

Mood Decides – Emotional Intelligence

You understand: anger, resentment, irritation, fear, excitement, arrogance are bad helpers in negotiations. And it doesn't matter if you are experiencing all this at the address of this particular interlocutor or whether something else hurt you. And not even related to this meeting. You have almost lost. Therefore, experienced negotiators recommend under any pretext to break off, restore lost balance, and only then continue the meeting—or replace with another negotiator. Sometimes, it is possible.

A good emotional tone in the negotiations is a light interest and a good background attitude to the interlocutor—the game is— moreover, the type where rates do not matter. We create this mood for ourselves—in advance and support in the process.

Take Care of Comfort

Any discomfort is distracting. Great discomfort distracts greatly. One woman lost the negotiations because she wanted to use the toilet. If you have an uncomfortable chair, or you feel like drinking or eating, or your shoes are shaking you, you yourself have put yourself in an uncomfortable position. If around it is noisy, smoky, cold, dark—this is a good reason to change the situation.

You have to take care of yourself! About your comfort—doubly. If the negotiations create uncomfortable conditions for you, to hell with such negotiations—all the same, they are already lost. You have the right to a comfortable environment. Comfort must be! Or you should have the skill to work where others are not comfortable working. Then, you have the advantage.

A small, fragile woman complained to the doctor of severe pain in the lower abdomen that occurs in her in wet and rainy weather. The doctor suggested she come to the reception when it would rain or snow, which she did. He invited her to lie down, and after a few seconds to get up and walk around the office.

"Well, how do you feel now?" The doctor asked.

- Perfectly! - answered the baby. "What did you do, doctor?"

"Nothing special," the doctor said embarrassedly. "I just cut off the tops of your boots for a couple of centimeters."

Prokaryote Search

You need to know yourself. All your weaknesses, fears, doubts. All shortcomings, inability, ignorance. All the dark and controversial moments of biography. In order not to be substituted. To know how to hide behind. To be able to compensate. To work out all the problem areas and become stronger and more perfect. To be ready.

Otherwise, everything is sad. And not before the game. And not up to comfort. And not until the implementation of the brilliant plan. Nothing.

When asked Chuck Norris how he became a karate champion, he replied that he analyzed his every defeat, found a weakness that made this defeat possible, and then went to the gym and trained to remove this weakness. Soon no one could defeat him.

Down with the Patterns

Some people always answer "no" to the first sentence. Some always answer yes to the fourth sentence. Alone, before making the biggest concession, some scratch their nose. Others start smoking every time they come across a surprise. Still, others always try to establish personal relationships with an opponent. If you have such stereotypes, you can be tackled. And replay to tackle your opponent. Conversely, identify your templates, get rid of your templates. Be free!

Indirect Exposure

Direct confrontation is stupid by definition—rigidity on rigidity, strength to strength, impudence on impudence, speed to speed. Here, the winner is the one who is tougher, stronger, bolder, faster, and in some places, dumber.

You need to win the mind. Influence the strong on the weak. Press where there is no resistance. Find the best ways to apply your efforts, and then the strength of your opponent will begin to work for you—and the stronger, tougher, bolder it is, the better it works.

The simplest thing we can do for this is to influence its internal factors—indirectly. Will we try?

Come On?

It is very good if you manage to start negotiations all of a sudden. Then, the other side will have no plan—neither will there be options and alternatives. They just had no time to think about all this! An experienced opponent will nevertheless set a goal, but what kind of goal this will be is also a question.

How do you implement this? You can try to make a working plan.

Sometimes, you can play with the appointment and cancellation of meetings. If you can push this, you can get a gorgeous tactical advantage. Then, even for meetings agreed in advance, he will not be able to prepare—or maybe not, but due to physical and emotional comfort. The end of the month, quarter, year, seasonal influx of customers, tax, and other checks—if you have the opportunity to find out such weakness and take advantage of it, then great!

Antidote? If the other side has come, and you are not ready yet, or even refuse to meet, referring to another employment—it is better to politely—or discuss only secondary issues and do not make clear promises. Option: get ready in advance.

Chapter 10:
When the Opponent Is a Manipulator

If the negotiating partner is a genius of communication, then it is best to find a way to make him or her replaced with a less talented one. Of course, this is possible in the sense that this person is not the decision-maker.

You can discredit. You can look for the possibility of transferring such a fellow to another project—preferably in another city. You can find him other life concerns.

Another good way is to find someone who can influence him. Now, I will write in more detail.

Golden Key

Someone is influencing each of us. Sometimes, someone's opinion is important; sometimes, the attitude; sometimes, the wishes—head, wife, lover, friend, a famous magazine, public opinion in the person of "Aunt Tasha," the cleaning lady.

If you can figure out people whose opinion is important for your future interlocutor, consider that you have already practically prepared the ground for negotiations—unless, of course, you can influence them.

And when they tell him about ten times from different sources how wonderful you are, how good it is to deal with you, how important it is to listen to your opinion and go towards you, you just have to appear and voice your proposal.

Become a Mythical Person

As we discussed earlier, experienced negotiators collect all available information about the other side. So make sure that all available information about you plays on you. Rumors, gossip, stories, legends—create a myth about yourself! And make it available to the masses. Plus, the reputation, of course, has not been canceled.

Let your opponents get conflicting, sometimes erroneous, mysterious information about you. Or they just gain the belief that you need to be friends, you need to be taken care of, cared for and cherished.

Arouse Emotions!

If you control emotions in a conversation, you control enough. You may have gaps in the argument and stretch in the logic. You may not have any normal rationale at all. If only it depended on you what the interlocutor will experience.

The ability to arouse interest, delight, joy, pleasure, curiosity, attraction, fear, doubt, insecurity, anger, disgust—this is all that is necessary for success in negotiations. If it is, the rest will follow.

If the interlocutor does not see the logic in your words, but he likes your ideas, he will come up with the logic himself. If the opponent does not agree with your arguments, but at the same time feels sadness and regret, he will be able to convince himself. Control your emotions, and you will succeed.

The State of the Interlocutor

It became clear that the creators were sitting here in the morning—in their eyes smoldered the light of the indescribable stupidity that the brain always emanates, exhausted by hours of brainstorming. - Anonymous.

It can also be influenced. Directly and indirectly. If you think of negotiations for your interlocutor's deadline, and he just doesn't physically have time to look for other options, his condition is good for you. Especially if you manage to pull the time politely. If this morning he was "accidentally" poured with mud over his car, he will not be very comfortable. If during a meeting with you they called him and told the good news, he will be more generous. If he holds a cup of roasting coffee poured to the top, part of his attention will be riveted to her.

Biorhythms, state of health, "random" meetings, background music, lack of sleep, day of the week—all this and much more affects the physical and psychological state of the interlocutor. And if you competently think about how to use all this, you can "make" even the best negotiator.

Pain Points, Weaknesses, Fears, Doubts

"Sir," a student asked, thinking, "how did you find out that she loves nuggets so much?"

"Learn to use the Internet, Daria," I explained. - A fool in the "interests" is everywhere written in plain text.

Any friends of his, old and new, information about the psychotype, observation of behavior and reactions—any strength has a dual weakness, so even laudatory reviews will tell you a lot. Just collect the information. We analyze. We are looking for optimal methods of exposure—because it would be wrong to use this information head-on. Only leave as a last resort.

Play on Weaknesses

Regrettably, the vast majority of people are cars. In the sense that they live quite mechanically. There is a stimulus—there will be a reaction. Press the button—you get the result. Already on this alone, you can build a huge number of effective manipulations.

Now, it is important for us that when you click on some buttons, people completely automatically give out stormy experiences. It is necessary to shout at someone, threaten another, praise the third, admire the fourth, show the fifth to the sixth, show the "sex-friendly" object, take the seventh away—of course, different things affect different people. Therefore, if the interlocutor did not give a significant reaction to one provocation, you need to move on to another.

To do this, you need to know the list of basic human weaknesses. For example, I offer these:

- Superiority

- Greed

- Pity

- Sex

- Patriotism

- Masculinity

- Femininity

- Fear

- Wine

- Generosity

- Envy

- Jealousy

- Justice

- "Weak?"

Over time, you will learn to determine by eye what this or that person will do. In the meantime, you can just do a bust. Or even switch to another way to set your interlocutor off balance for your antics to work.

We Are Not Robots; Robots Are Not We

Information collection is standard. We are looking for patterns in the spirit of, "In the situation 'X,' he acts 'U.'" Accordingly, we can provoke the "U" we need by creating the corresponding "X." For example, when they praise his car, he blurs with a happy smile. Clearly, what needs to be done to make him smile? If he agrees only to the third proposal, the first two cannot be soared. And the third is to make it profitable for us.

On the other hand, if we know what external signs are responsible for what internal reaction, we actually "read the thoughts" of the interlocutor—which is convenient. Look for patterns!

Territory Development

They say that special forces differ from ordinary well-physically and psychologically trained troops in only one: the completeness and quality of information about the enemy and the place of the future massacre. Under this information, a model of the future theater of operations is built. Then, tactical combat schemes are planned and practiced to be automatic. Therefore, special forces and is able to destroy many times superior enemy, and even on its territory.

If the information is false, the special forces are doomed. And no hand-to-hand combat with mark shooting helps them—foreign territory.

The funny thing is that many people go to important "meetings" with them, not even having mastered their own territory. What really does fit into any framework, you should still propose to master it.

The Best Alternative to Negotiations

- Remember, Daria: the manager's authority is not based on what he successfully said, but on what he successfully did. The more you do, the more they will offer you next time. Learn to send, Daria! Learn to make a decision about sending it! This is a vital skill. Until you master it—you do not master the profession, everyone will use you. And you should use all, on the contrary, you!

If negotiations fail, what will happen to you? Where are you going to go? Who to contact? A simple fact: if the alternatives you have are the sea, you are calm, like a boa constrictor, easily take risks and can play on the verge of a foul. And the attitude arises—that same game. If you have a rich choice, you will not put up with the inconvenience. If there is no choice, you will have to come to terms. If you have nothing to fear, you will not use harsh and ugly methods. People pressed against the wall are capable of any meanness.

Look for alternatives! Expand your selection! Explore the market. Offer to many. And when the price of defeat falls, there will be significantly more victories.

Let the Walls Help You

"Maybe I should not go to the palace?"

- How to walk! Sorrel raised his voice. "I will need a henchman."

- A henchman?

- Well, yes. One who listens to me — err, cast spells — and admires them: the very first degree of apprenticeship.

It is good when it depends on us where we will meet with the interlocutor! After all, we can make everything play for us. Or a lot. The ideal situation is when the territory is fully developed by you but is not familiar to him at all. Then, you have almost won.

If everyone around you shows honor, the interlocutor inevitably imbues with respect. If the music that helps to create the right mood sounds, it's also good. If it depends on you what will be served on the table, you have an advantage. If everything that happens does involuntarily distract his attention, and you are used to it, everything is just wonderful.

The appearance and disappearance of certain people. Calls to mobile. Shine. Music. Furniture. Create an atmosphere! And do not forget about your own convenience. Let your acquaintance psychologist sit next door—he will tell you how to behave and point out mistakes. Let convenient access to the Internet be nearby if you need quick reference information. Let your friend be here, next to whom you will be "knee-deep in the sea of affairs." The territory is a creative affair.

Who Is Around?

If your support group is around, with an approving hum that meets all your remarks and is ready to boo any creep in your direction, the opponent will be hard.

Anyway, no matter who is nearby, it is sometimes more useful to influence the interlocutor through the audience. Very often, speakers do not turn to the opponent, who will object anyway, but to the public, which will support it sooner. Let your words and actions look beautiful. Attractive. And well, if he himself will be shy of his actions. Witnesses determine!

Therefore, by the way, it can be useful to invite rude negotiators with their wives—for a dinner party, for example. And then, they automatically lose all the advantages of the usual style of communication—against the background of a man who, in theory, should have played on his side.

Leeway

Everything is clear here: we create the maximum margin of time for ourselves and adjust to the minimum margin for the other side. Then, we are calm, and time plays on us. And the opponent twitches. Because time is playing against him.

We have already discussed this.

Where Is the World Heading?

Where are oil prices moving? What is the situation with the labor market? Where does the political course go? What major competitors will enter the market soon? And if you know what market is, political, cultural, etc. situations will play on you at some point, you can guess.

Laws, Concepts, Customs, Rules

Lawyers live by this: they find the rules confirming the correctness of the clients. And the fact that a good lawyer can find arguments in favor of almost any side clearly demonstrates that you need to know the laws.

It is useful to know your rights. It is useful to know the responsibilities of others. To make you comply with the law. Or at least just what you need now.

Master the territory.

Win-Win

The described approaches to preparing for negotiations may suggest that the meaning of any negotiations is to squeeze the opponent dry. This is *not* true. I still hold the idea that leaving behind grateful people is better than leaving behind offended ones. It's more useful for business—yes, and for health.

I have seen more than once how masters and "monsters" of negotiations received "feedback" for abuse of their negotiating talent. They left them, quarreled with them, and betrayed them— and they did not even understand why. Therefore, it is best to build relationships with people in a spirit of mutual benefit: win-win.

However, in order to do this, you need to control the situation— to be the master in it, to navigate. And from this situation, it is entirely possible to bless the partner with mutually beneficial conditions—and he *will* be grateful.

Another thing is if you, without any influence on the situation, will timidly bleat on the topic of mutual benefit—the smart ones will smile and "swipe you crumbs from the master's table." Stupid—just laugh. And if in the same situation, you decide to make a generous gesture yourself, no one will appreciate it. Just take it for granted—by right of the strong.

And it is right. Since a person costs just as much as he appreciates himself—so let's value ourselves highly, take power into our own hands, and dispose of it correctly—so that people remain grateful to us. And with pleasure, they want to cooperate further.

Conclusion

In the single structure of the impact on which this book is built, the synchronization stage has begun. All the necessary suggestions have already been given. All training demonstrations have been produced. Your unconscious has received its tasks for practicing—and even for the latent period, some parts were used.

Of course, I won't be able to stop you from immediately re-reading this book again, wondering at how clearly and openly I acted here—and the fact that many things the first time you did not notice. But still, I ask: wait a while. Let your unconscious have a couple of months of odds. Let amnesia work where necessary. Then, catch up—if you want.

I can only invite you to communicate further through books. I am happy to read your reviews, successful reports, etc..

Remember: learn what to do with yourself and not with others.

Good luck!